Equatorial Derbyshire

by

Paul Devon Young

Equatorial Derbyshire

Text Copyright

© 2021 Paul Devon Young

All Rights Reserved

The factual parts of this account are as the author had understood and perceived the events and experiences. Other people involved may have experienced events differently.

NOTE:
This book has explicit content and is
not for consumers under 18.

Published via pgprintandofficeservices.co.uk

Cover design collaboration: dartworks.design

Front Cover Photo © Sandy Brown

Author's Notes

1

I had to alter the narrative to approach the personal subject matters from an abstract viewpoint, so I re-wrote certain areas and the subject matters, or took them out completely once I found a way to maintain the narrative.

There are subject matters that I could not alter, change or re-arrange, but overall I feel the landscape [layout] is smooth.

The expression has become overall softer, the weight lifted from the book.

An abstract jazz frequency now moves through it, which is what I sought from the start with the reference to Oscar Peterson.

2

What I have replaced some paragraphs or viewpoints with is an abstract directness viewed or interpreted as a child would – the eyes of a young person, the directness, makes them more potent, in an abstract way – yes we know it, but won't say it...

3

Also, the lingua in the book...

I just thought about how this mother tongue always slips in conversations. For example, the spelling of my name Paul, and the pronunciation at home... the sound Paaal was meant for Paul. The 'u' never entered, or was replaced by more 'a's... so I have used home lingua mostly throughout the book... the way mother would speak ... I speak also.

Also the way mother could easily switch to middle English on the phone always made me pay attention to how the outside world spoke...

4

It took a bit of time to let the book go.

I had feelings about letting it go, felt I wasn't ready.

Ready for what?

To let the book go...

Any particular reason?

Yeah... why do we do it, eh?

Do what?

Seek the me factor. Who really cares about stinking drawers? Seems everyone does, and that's the point.

Well, here goes...

Good luck...

Now I am really ready to hand over for print...

~

Just to make a sound for everyone who helped in one way or another...

Brothers, sister, aunts, uncles, cousins.

Friends and family,

I wish you all good health...

Our world family...

And lastly – cormorant.

Big up your chest to Jupiter or Neptune.

But not Pluto... yet...

Why not Pluto?

~

Also, I would like to share with you a brief memory...

The Mountain was running.

As I ran alongside it, I asked,

"Why you running?"

"I'm not running," replied the Mountain.

If it seems, it's not...

~

Wait, wait... we need to start the book...

Okay, I can see there's definitely an issue here; you still haven't handed the book over...

When does it start, or are we half way through?

No, no, we are still on page one.

I'm expressing a crisis on iPad.

It's not that...

Well, what is it this time?

I'll have him, poison him, burn him on the fridge, that weird young freak.

That's the shit reason I haven't handed the book over.

The black community won't like it...

They'll call me a demon, a *battyman*.
I'll have to hide. Oh fuck, this is no joke.

Let me at him
Let me at him
Let me at him

Let you at what?

I already told you,
that faggot that took advantage.

This pile o' shit is going on the fire.
Publishing what?
Yu mad? Ar [or] *tuppid?*
Can you imagine the children hearing such talk...
No, no, no...
I will not publish...

Paul, I listen to you, and I suppose it's your decision.
Publishing the book, what you put in the book; you must feel comfortable with its content.
Also, the book, it's for adults, not children.

Paul, I can tell you this: the black community embrace all people of good character regardless of sexuality.

Which black people dat? Some don't like em.

It's an ingrained thing.
They quote the Bible.

And that's the point, Paul.
You were young, not even 12 yet.

Do you think you have really accepted what happened over
a period of time, as you shared dormitories?
Be gentle on yourself now. Remember.

Listen... it sounds like the book has started.

The book started a long time ago, it's not new.

Neither are the cobwebs.

I wrote about it in the book.

I told you, I'm trying to work it out.

It's big, those whispers,

Nettle stingers.

*Please forgive me for allowing this to happen and not
reacting in any way to it but by being still...*

It's hell for sure, child or not.

The thing is, I keep seeing his face now.

After all these years I can see him clearly...

He had issues on the autistic spectrum.

He had this kind of frenzied smile.

*Tall and thin... that fukin' nastiness him put pon mi nah
abide good.*

Is prees [priest] *mi ah look fi nung...*

Prees

Prees

*Prees, how much yu chaarg fi di cleansin body fram
nastiness?*

7

Child, it depends upon the sin. What happened? What sin have you committed this time?

This time? How you mean? This time?
Is me com fi di cleansin, yu see any beast roun ya?

Speak up, what is the sin?

Does it have to be sin?
Can't it just be an incident instead?

No, son. It's sin for sure.

Born in sin is how this thing works...

Works?
What thing?

Do you need cleansing from sin?

How much is it?

It's free.
I will pray for you and that's it...

Thank you.

What did I expect?
It's just how it is, and so I will put it away for a while and see if I can work this issue out as I still feel mixed up about it...

Mixed up about sharing such weird context and at the same time it wants to come out...

Where's that faggot now? I'll have him...

I'll, I'll, I'll, I'll screeeem at him and curse him... and then I'll say sorry, I'm mixed up.

Could I have prevented it?

Why didn't I tell a teacher?

Well, there was a teacher just outside the door doing night duty who would come in if anything happened.

Obviously not in my case.

They would have known. Yes, they knew, but allowed it as experimental experience...

They would reason it as not being gender based but just experimental.

Paul, does this help?

Yu tink yard bwoi hago siddung an listen dis chat yah?

No sah, im hago trow rockstone an sen fya pon u raas.

Dem man deh nuh easi, nuh easi ta raas.

But true to the matter, some will reason it as past wrong-doing and let it go...

What do you mean, past wrong-doing?

When it's measured right, it was an act not understood by the participant so he cannot be held responsible for it.

The fact that he has to come to terms with it and move on in whichever way he chooses will be his acceptance of the matter.

Anyone who disagrees with this measure must consider their own judgements...

~

And so with this and all the content the book shall go to print...

Thanks for your patience...

~

No...

Rolled in a ball tight, tight, holding on to what seems like eternity, timeless, the ball so, so tight, then I seem him...

I'll have him... I'll have him.

Hold me back someone...

I'll have him.

What will you have? We've passed it all. Case closed.

Nuh worry yu self

De ting dun

Ire out man

Satta

Ole down a lami

Some ginga tonic

And so... finally I can hand the book over for print...

Look, something's happened.

You've turned it into pantomime.

No one's interested now...

Dis book ya ting...

Is juss lavish talk ah gwaan, but mi like di nun part eena di convent. That part sweet. Me good. What an experience, eh? She mussi know seh yu nuh teef nar robba fi me kyu keep di fruits.

10

The Trial of Character

Stand up please, Mr Paul Devon Young.
Can you answer the question I will put before you?

Yes, to my greatest knowing of the matter...

You say you weren't rogered, rammed from behind?
Is this so?

Yes, it is so.

Were you ever an active participant in these demonic acts?

[I knew it. I knew they would speak like this.]
Do you mean am I part of the school cult?

Well no, not willingly nor unwillingly.

You're protecting that faggot, for sure.

Why do you use such terms as faggot? Are you not ashamed
to be calling fellow human beings such derogatory terms?

I'm not interested in terms. I want that faggot... where is
he?

Looking at these reports, it seems you are stuck with the
terms...
...Faggot.
...Let me have him.
...I'll, I'll, I'll...

Are you on medication?

No.

Has your GP suggested any?

What for?

To help the thought patterns, break them up. So you're not going round and round...

It's not as simple as that. What I need is to speak with him, find out why he did what he kept doing.

I don't even know for how long he did it as he came a lot, when I think about it.

...and King Shilluk knew all along...

I'll have King Shilluk.

Let me have him, let me have him.

King Shilluk, you're on trial next...

~

On one strange level, the 'trial' proved that:

1. I was not a part of any cult.
2. Neither did I willingly participate in any carnal activity, and lastly...
3. That I am not anti-gay, as the media put it.

I have stated in many previous interviews that I have no issues with gays nor lesbians.

Look, I don't want to judge anyone.

I'm not a judge.

I see people in their fullness.

Do you know what it's like to be seen in one's fullness?

The little dogmatic trappings fall away.

The conversation becomes whole.

When you finally did see him after all these years, what happened?

What was the feeling?

Well, he was an old man,

Thin and wiry.

I didn't even recognise him.

I was informed that he had been on medication all his life for many things, including psychosis.

We didn't talk. He barely looked at me.

It was an experiment that went wrong.

Wrong from the well-intentioned start...

But I had to learn to forgive myself, and not see it from a blaming, black and white viewpoint...

Man, wherever you are, is juss love...

~

ATAVIST

The reappearance of a characteristic in an organism after several generations of absence...

...related to the attitudes and behaviour of the first humans.

SILENT INCANTATION TO ALL NATIONS OF THE WORLD... A SILENT INCANTATION FOR GRATITUDE

A POEM

This poem was written in 2007 whilst staying on a farm in North Devon.

It was February and the snow was blowing.

I decided to go for an evening stroll and was walking along the country lane, the same country lane I took that little young cockerel for a walk when it was being bullied by the other cockerels; on this farm it was my job to feed the geese, the cows and the fowl... *back to the poem soon.*

Well, the young cockerel was bullied by the older ones.

I observed that the older cockerels would rather go without food but that new young one was not eating.

It wasn't a matter of letting them sort it out as they attacked him every time; it stood no chance of eating as there were four other cockerels, this one making five. I thought, if only they could put him in a shed alone, so I took him for a walk along the same lane as in the poem. The cockerel stayed close by as there were no cars passing.

We didn't go too far, just a stretch along the lane. When we came back and I opened the gates, the other cockerels didn't bother him at all, as I observed.

I called it chicken therapy when recalling it, as we both benefited from it.

Back to the poem...

It was on this lane in 2007 that I walked that cold winter evening.

As I approached the end of the lane and onto the Atlantic Highway, the storm was wild – snow and wind blowing and howling, bleak with an eerie light darkness.

I looked up the bleak highway.

I looked down the bleak highway.

Then the poem came...

THE STONE

The stone belongs to no particular season
But reminds me still of
Spring summer autumn winter

The stone belongs to no one
And yet we gather it
Embrace it
Seek memory from it
O stone unturned
Await not the light of darkness
Nor the blessings of decay.

~

Dear Oscar Peterson,

What a gift you are both musically and as a person, which are one.

Every time I see you play, those fingers making sublime music on the piano, I thank the elements for your eternal frequency...

The 9 elements of mother earth.

~

A TALKING RIVER...

AFRICA, WHAT IS OUR TRUE NAME?

ABULAN – AWENDA, AWENDA, AWENDA

INTRODUCTION

This book is an autobiographical account of my time experienced as a child to teenager at a Special Residential School in rural Derbyshire.

I had lived in this school from the mid-'70s to early '80s.

Also woven into the story are pieces of my maternal parents, mainly my mother's input into my life and how this invaluable input also shaped it prior to going to live in this residential school.

I have mentioned my father's input much later when I met him for the first time as a teenager of 14 years old.

Also, there are extracts from the ghetto – the urban ways that I encountered before and after leaving the school care system.

I have written the book in a way where the reader will be in many locations – school, home, teenage years and present, but the narrative is consistent with the theme of society – strata.

Because of the way I have written it, there are no chapters.

Just headings to keep the narrative tight. For example – 'Back to school' as a heading, means that I went off into explaining a subject relating to a subject related to school but now I am specifically back to school...

All that is written I have had a direct experience of on one level or the other.

I chose to write this story a long time ago; it kept coming back to me, all those experiences with the other children... the staff.

It kept coming back to me and I still didn't fit in, even with my artwork – more on that later.

I did have a few scribbles from the past waiting for one day to write the book!

~

I was eventually encouraged to write the book by an old lady called Valerie.

We had built up a relationship travelling on the same bus every week for 13 years.

Valerie was late 70s, me mid-50s.

We really enjoy our time together. Valerie told me all about her life: her parents, her brother, her late husband, how they lived in the '40s, '50s, '60s, '70s and so on. What we realised one day when I got on the bus...

"It's my birthday today," said Valerie.

"Really! It's mine too."

We both laughed, her in her deep Devon accent; you wouldn't have thought she came out of suburban Surrey to rural Devon in the mid '40s when 2 years of age.

When I told Valerie one day on my way to the workshop of my plans to write a book, she laughed.

"Gonna be rich, ar ye?"

We both laughed.

But overall Valerie thought it was a good way to share my story.

I still see Valerie on the bus and her brother has just published a book about their family coming down from suburban Surrey to back-bush rural Devon.

Valerie now walks with a stick, being early 80s. In the past 13 years Valerie has not changed much and is a true historian of the shires. I love just to hear her talk; she's very clued-up and witty.

She recalls the cottage that they lived in on the estate. Her father was the main gardener and the cottage came with the job.

She explains that he failed his medical test for the army and had a temper at times.

The mother was used to suburban life and struggled to adapt to basic rural living.

Valerie recalls when her cousins, her mother's sister and children, came to stay the children would mock and laugh at the Devon accent.

Likewise the Devon rural kids would laugh at their Surrey accents, which soon took a back seat as Devon embraced them totally, which is evident when Valerie speaks.

~

Then I realised my spelling was still not that good if not checked. I had the ideas but putting them down was not easy as some words were spelt wrong. Luckily, I had a small laptop that corrected my spelling of most words. This gave me confidence to proceed, so slowly I peeled back those green years of my childhood youth in rural Derbyshire and beyond.

Once I started the script, the laptop keys made the book flow naturally. My memory was clear on most incidents and different ideas... there's so much.

I want to put together a narrative of the school and how we lived.

For instance, I recall music every morning and a certain boy continually slumping to the floor and passing out; it wasn't epilepsy but something to do with nose bleeds.

We would be talking, then his nose would bleed and he would just drop right next to or in front of me.

We had each other as brothers and the staff as parents.

I liked being outside a lot, so was in the right environment to see the night sky with stars in them.

Before you go...

As a person first, some say colour comes with identity.

The complexity of race, particularly the term black race, it's too vast, the interpretation of self in historic context, a sense of place.

Culture, for example...

A boy brought a drum home. His whole family looked at him in amazement.

"Dad, dad, I got a drum."

"Son, we not in the jungle no more. We use mobile phones now..."

The boy's face fell. The drum was his mobile phone...

So he took it upstairs and started to tap on it.

The sound that came back caused him to beat the drum a little harder, quicker. Soon he was in a steady bush groove.

The dogs started barking.

His mother came off the phone and went upstairs.

"Bwoi, stap dat foolishness...
we nuh eena trouble,
drum ha trouble pikni
mek jesus yu drum pikni - fallo him riddim,
an stap dat nastiness..."

22

The boy looked at his mother. Her face was like a pear, oval-like. Thick black long plaited hair.

Was she hiding something from him?

Why was the drum trouble?

He pressed his mother over food.

"Mama? Why di drum trouble?"

"Dem nuh really like e..."

"Who dem?"

"Cho... nyam yu yood. Yu axs too much questan... jess like yu sista Penelope, who always ah fuss wid big words... mussi di nyam mi gi ar..."

THE STARS

Whenever I look at the sky, day or night, I see shapes, figures. At first when I saw them I kept quiet, but in the latter years when I told someone, they thought I was confused as they could not see the shapes, or colours.

Sometimes they are right in your face, but these are timeless kin travelling though multi dimensions like we always have...

During this read you will encounter many an incident of what could be called *natural phenomena*.

For example, in 2015 I was working processing some pigments. I sat with the sun in front of me.

At my right side I felt a light frequency and could recognise a fluid figure, like a fluid crystal form; it was trying to get my attention, but on this occasion I decided to keep working.

Sometimes I just be still.

As I decided to keep working, the crystal form kind of went under my face and to the side of me as I looked on.

The frequency was uplifting, calm, benign, with clarity.

The school evoked something in me that has a direct link to my elemental works. On leaving the school at 16, not yet reading or writing that well, I recall the starkness of society.

Gone was the green; in with the grey.

Having to adapt to a society where race, class, stereotypes all come charging at you full speed.

How did I focus it?

From a sheltered environment to a cesspit called estate, or the Shitty as je préfère.

Whereby I was immediately expected to hustle, fight, do drugs and be the man everyone was, in one way or another, and if you didn't fit into any group they target you as an outsider, informer – stranger, battyman, *eediat* – all these come charging at you by the same people you thought you had some connection with, but in reality one will see it for what it really is...

Trine ta find a way in da shitty became an artform of expression.

It's how it went. Some called it Ghetto Fabulous – with lavish clothes, hair and dance.

Groups within groups all hustling one way or other.

In a way it was quick wit hustle, but some were so elaborate and organised you wouldn't know it.

For example, walking down a street you could be confronted to buy drugs, say crack.

The fact you say no or don't reply could cause attention, commotion, so you were always aware of where you were going; it was a maze of no, nos.

Some of the fights I witnessed were over nothing, but fights all the same broke out every day, whether in groups or singles.

Now this chapter needs some sensible vocale [attention]...

It's the queenies – the young female teens of the Shitty...

In reality they control the whole thing.

I got to know some close as friends and although sometimes they would hang with the guys, they were always doing their own things, which attracted the boys, so the boys followed them...

Mostly I recall the banter. It was full of wit but potent at the same time.

For example, I brought a female friend onto the Shitty and Samantha – queenie – says, "She walks like she don't shit." My friend heard it and never came back.

Samantha...

She had biggish eyes, tight lips and a cute face, almost mask-like, regal, but she had a mouth on her...

She had a group of female friends that had stuck together from birth .

Nothing bad, just a tight group of queens of mixed races.

When I knew them they were around 15 to 17 years of age.

They were like women already.

I remember one who had saved money.

I asked her why she saved. She always said it's good to save money, which I never took in, but even then, right there in the Shitty, the race war was being played out.

Many people had relationships, not realising the consequences, as in reality, if I remember, mixed race was not seen as good. There were names like half-caste, which totally knocked me out for years.

I honestly was looking for two castes of a person, and when I looked and saw one caste I got even more confused.

When the latter term mixed race stepped in...

Let me re-phrase that, when the up-market term mixed race stepped in, half-caste was vacated to far flung Siberia, never to be mentioned again, apart from here.

So it was the case suddenly of mixed relationships not realising race was involved, which hasn't changed one bit, it's still a bit like – guess who's coming to dinner.

I feel friendships and understanding has come leaps and bounds even from the start, the start of my mother coming to England and being a host [Windrush immigrant].

"Are we hosts too, Mami?"

Well, all this was played out in the Shitty and so even being still could get you in trouble; you had to look like you were doing something, just act something out like painting a wall...

~

I recall a song by one of the greatest vocalists of all time.

The track is called 'Hard Times' by Curtis Mayfield.

This song can do more for consciousness and awareness of troubles in the Shitty...

It's a beautiful reminder, telling you directly how it is.

Back to intro...

My concern mainly is black-on-black crime; this is the real issue that most people refuse to tackle.

How did I deal with the fast-talking hustlers?

Police officers?

Jobs – adapting. It was all too quick.

Eye contact – this was an issue. I found it difficult most of the time to make eye contact or would look straight past people.

THE KMT LOOK

I remember growing up and seeing this stern look on the black men's faces, mainly the older ones, but also the middle-aged and some younger youth. Why this expression? It was permanently fixed. I was soon to realise myself why this expression was there. These KMT men were being made to feel uncomfortable, intimidated even, in their neighbourhood...

The race mongers – Nationalists.

Society strata.

Where's my place in all of this?

Identity – where do I belong?

Shitty Green.

Why shitty?

Why yu still ere?

Aint we rich yet?

Aint we spose to be on equal opportunities, jess like dem migrant workers that drink in Cecil's den, I seen em staggering out.

One got twerked really bad, even the ambulance wouldn't come.

It's no use, I'll have to ask Mami.

Mamiiiii.

Mamii

Mami comin'.

"Mami, why wi still eena di shitty?"

"Mi pikni yu afi mek good outa bad, yu cyaan fine fault eena everiting."

"Cah yu have uptown shitty an down town shitty? Dem is all shitty."

"Soh nu feel seH yu cyan step fram shitty cah is di peeple dem whom mek di shitty shitty. Yu tink shitty cyan mek shitty owta wind. Noh sah mi pikni... memba dat."

NOTES ON THE NO FACTOR

The no factor? This was and is one of the hardest hurdles in society.

You didn't know why people kept saying no to you most of the time and yes to a next man. This applied in most aspects.

When I spoke to my mother about this in the late '90s, she told me I needed to work 4 times harder to achieve anything.

Well mother, I've worked the 4 times harder, maybe 10 times harder, but I realised whilst working 10 times harder no one cared, only you.

And the sun and the moon and the stars shine on...

[Home grown lingua]

Rhatid cup - Cup ah rhatid...

The imbecile badge attached to my employment files.

More on this later as this label really affected my outlook on society, once I realised it was there.

Or even continually being stopped for just existing.

This happened a lot back then and really hasn't changed. It's psychological racism, and if that didn't exist you wouldn't have black police officers themselves complaining of racism.

It's an illness imposed on you from a young age.

This and many more incidents I have recorded to share with society as a reflection.

So, from the rolling hills of equatorial Derbyshire, I present to you my accounts of time spent there and beyond.

The mask is clay
Cooked in the oven
It is an identity
Not yours though…

Paul Devon Young

To Describe Maurice...

A cross between Curtis Mayfield and Courtney Pine in facial and body features.

Maurice was a little chubby, with his round face and glasses, and such a delicate, gentle soul.

I remember one time going home for the weekend and I sat with him on the bus.

He had a raspy voice, I recall, and would have been around 14.

I didn't know he had a keen interest in antique cars, but an old classic car overtook us and Maurice exploded.

"Look at that car. Look at that car." He almost pasted himself onto the window.

I never saw Maurice react like this before.

The Eternal Message

Every morning we would stand in the big hall and sing songs.

The headmaster, Mr Hooper, informed us one morning that Maurice was no longer with us and wouldn't be coming back. He had passed away with his illness.

It was a sad message, although most of us did not understand it, but we knew he was gone.

THE SCHOOL

Hopwell Hall Special Residential School –
for children with emotional learning difficulties

I lived at this school for 5 years, from 1976 to 1981, and this was our home where we all lived and played together.

In 2004 I tried with a friend to find the school online.

Luckily we did and took the information from the web. The next time we searched for the school it had completely gone.

Well, the above description is about right, but in 2020 I found new references to the school and it mentions Mr Gregory. I feel so happy to see his name there. He was one of my favourite teachers.

It seems that the information on the school is protected as I tried to find out more about it. Well, I found enough...

~

It was an idyllic setting in Derbyshire where the soil and seasons were the cycle, the pace of life. It was slow yet full of things to do.

The vastness of the views always kept me preoccupied as my mind stretched into the distant echoes of past valleys, times and peoples.

The green openness was very hot in the summer, very white and cold in the winter.

As the seasons were so clearly distinct, I got familiar with them.

I remember the winter fires outside, and sledging endlessly, building igloos with help, and snowball fights.

I liked the snow so much it was hard to keep me inside.

The cold didn't bother us one bit as the teachers tried to keep jackets on us.

I remember the early dark skies of winter.

The clouds were still and vast, overlaying one another with no edges.

The tall cedars and sycamores, spruces and oaks stood tall, some naked. Not the evergreens, though; they were always covered in green.

At the side of the farm were a cluster of trees, almost like a mini forest but scattered. Sometimes when you went in there the woodpecker would be busy at work.

I got so familiar with that sound. When I heard ochre being addressed this morning, maybe 15 years later, it took me back to the woods.

Snakes. We had a few adders that made a fuss one day when the chickens tried to attack one, thinking it was a large worm maybe?

Well, one day we found some slow-worms in the barns and asked the teacher about them. I remember Mr Gordon saying that the slow-worm is not a snake and can be a pet. Since there were a lot of them, we would play with them in summer a lot.

Spring...

I was born in spring and look forward to the changes.

All the winter flowers are in flux and spring was summoned by its bloom.

THE BUILDINGS

When I found the school online and saw its presence, for a while I didn't connect with it.

It took some time as it was big.

The building had a distinct presence.

Although the building was kept warm, certain areas remained cold. I used to stand in them to make sure and, yes, it was cold in that area, warm in the rest of the room.

I found this in a number of places in the building.

It had long, dark halls, mostly lit up, but overall dark due to its décor, which was all shades of brown...

What is it with these stately homes and brown paint?

Well, it had a homely presence and lots of functional rooms.

One time I was going to collect some boots from the sports hall cupboards and I heard a fluttering and looked around. I couldn't see anything so I went to the cupboard and then I saw it...

It was a completely orange bird with sea blue eyes. It just sat there on the post frame looking out, not at me.

I assumed it was a local bird that had flown in and would find its way out. But the windows were high and looked shut. The door was closed as well.

Once I got my boots and was coming out of the small room, the bird was still sitting on the same spot.

I thought to tell a teacher, and went a bit closer to look at the bird.

It had this unusual feeling about it.

It seemed, the closer I got to it, I was aware that my body felt almost like fluid and I went to move back. At this precise moment of thought, the bird slowly came off the post and flew straight past me, very close, almost touching my shoulder, then straight through the wall.

It all happened so quickly and yet slowly, as I had time to see it all, but it was fast as well.

I remember going straight outside, and looked for the orange bird for weeks. I never saw it again, but I did remember.

Looking back now, anyone watching would have deemed me crazy...

I remember the dreams I had, as they were repeated for a long while.

This was one the most vivid as it followed me from the coal bunker to the dormitory.

THE DREAM

Because this dream was repetitive I got to know the location very well and was familiar with sounds and smells, not forgetting the dust...

I always, when in the dream, found myself amongst zebras, really close.

It was the stark black and white I observed as they were still and I would hear their sounds as they communicated.

It was always hot and hazy and I would awake with the blanket off me.

Amongst these zebras, I was a child, just standing taking in the scene or landscape, which was vast and empty, with a mountain in the distance. Apart from this, that's all I ever saw, how they all huddled together, then stampeded, then calm again.

I took keen notice of their ears, nose, mouth, hind legs, but mostly their alertness.

They were so aware of their environment.

Then there would be a stampede and all hell broke loose. I would stay in the same place, watching all the stripes together creating psychedelic patterns alongside the red dust.

How the bodies twisted, contorted the heads; tails, legs flown in all directions, all in black and white stripes...

I remember telling my mother about it, as it was happening most of the time.

As a child, I think she said something like,

"That's nice..."

But when I was still having the same dreams later and I told her, she didn't say anything like the first time, but spoke to my grandmother, Ma P. who told mother to send me to her so she could raise me, but mother couldn't afford the fare.

~

I didn't realise it, but I was being abused, not sexually, but physically and mentally, by grown-ups.

This had a massive impact on my view of adults, even now as an adult.

It is only the atavist essence that can deal with life's contradictions, as they are a part of me, alongside common-sense.

~

In the latter years of 2000, I asked my mother about the school and why I went there.

My mother informed me that I had seen some child specialists at the age of 7 who informed her that my IQ was lower than a 2-year-old's.

That warranted many changes to follow, alongside abuse.

More on that later...

This also was part of the reason why I ended up in the boarding school.

When away from my mother, she also informed me that she tried to get me back home, but the abuse was still lurking.

That is why I had to live with different families until I attended the residential school...

I also recall an experience prior to going into care...

We were all in bed, me and my younger brother. He was fast asleep, but I was wide awake. Suddenly, there was a shadow on the wall, but you could see the details of it, even the features. The figure had a top hat and a waistcoat with a little watch attached to the waistcoat. What got me pelting down the stairs was his pipe, as the smoke trickled from it, slowly filling the room. I was gone...

When my mother brought me upstairs, the first thing she said was, "Who's been playing with matches?" to switch my mind from it, but it didn't work. He had a distinct, chubby face with bulbous eyes, quite a calm gentleman's presence.

Back to the school building...

There were lots of outer buildings plus a big main entry hall.

The name Hopwell Hall suggests some bygone stately place.

Even then I was aware of the big building and its big old beams. All those buildings seemed to have a lot of brown décor and an old lost era smell.

Also the windows were wide and high and the sun shone through in the mornings, overlooking the vast dales.

Rising in the mornings was fun. You would get up, pull all sheets back, go for a wash (the staff would be there to assist if needs be), then onto breakfast which was in the vast dining room hall.

Mr Hooper was the headmaster. It felt odd to sit at the head table with him.

On a few occasions I was told to sit there for, say, breakfast or lunch.

It was a quiet meal, as we focused on the food.

When we sat together, we talked all the time.

The hall had a distinct smell as it was in front of the kitchen so it always had a smell of familiar meals – the kitchen was the homely zone.

Back to the table...

Mr Hooper was a big man.

If I had to go to his office when he called for me for anything, before he opened his mouth, I would bellow out loud, and that would be that.

One time I climbed out of his window, I was so frightened of him, although he never put a finger on me.

He was a big man, with a deep voice, and when I knew he wanted to see me, the bellow would come.

He would just look at me and retreat, as it was a genuine bellow of deep stress. This was normal... when you've been battered from birth and you have issues alongside that.

~

The old barns were always places to play in, with the sturdy wooden steps leading to the loft, a favourite spot for day-dreaming.

It was also the place where the fowl would hang out.

I would sometimes watch them from this high spot as they were always looking for something I couldn't see.

CLASSROOMS AND LESSONS

I can vaguely remember our structured lessons – cooking... carpentry... reading and writing... spelling... gardening... farm work... Morris dancing... sports...

The lessons were on a rota. I can't remember which days we had lessons, but each lesson was carried out in a classroom or sports hall, outdoor depending on what lesson we had.

I remember singing and story-time being held in the hall.

Singing and Cooking, which I enjoyed a lot, was taught by Mrs Gregory.

Mr and Mrs Danes were both tall people. He was big and sturdy. I don't recall having lessons with him but I do recall his big presence.

He could have been a Danish giant in his previous job. His wife was one of the matrons. I recall Mrs Danes as a mother figure, very warm with the clarity of grounding those matrons have...

A scrape, a nettle sting, whatever you had, the matrons would cure it, if you let them.

CLOTHING

If I remember, we had uniforms but no jacket, just shorts, shirt and jumper, with black shoes.

I was fond of my shoes and would study them: the soles, the smell of the leather, the repeats of the same black shoes in many different sizes. Likewise jumpers and trousers...

I don't recall ever wearing a hat there, and was comfortable with the clothes we had.

Someone had to wash them all every week, lots and lots of children's clothes...

If we had a tear in our clothes or a button fell off, we would go to the matron's laundry room...

[Home lingua]

What ah pappi show.

THE MATRON'S LAUNDRY ROOM

It was the place where all the domestics were done, a large room with long tables in the middle full of pens, tape, needles, sewing machines, etcetera.

The walls had huge, old, wooden panels filled with socks, shirts, jumpers, trousers and other things.

It was always warm, quite noisy and full of matrons.

It had this distinct pine polish smell with some faint perfume that even the furniture used to emit.

Looking back now, it was a place I tried to avoid as they always kept you for a long time.

If you went in for anything, you were aware of their presence and tried to get out quickly, but they would always keep you longer. "Just a measurement there, Paul. Let's get you some new shoes, Paul." It was all fun, though.

Mr Hooper's wife was one of the matrons. A tiny woman, very fashionable and motherly.

Mrs Hooper was always around, with her two children who also lived on the premises.

It's odd to think back that the headmaster actually lived on the premises, although I do remember their house at the back and to the side. Sometimes I would look at it and wonder.

In the entry hall, on the school wall, were photographs in black and white of the previous year's pupils. I think some photos went back to the 1930s.

I remember really taking them in, each face, as much as possible, as if some connection takes place.

There were rows and rows of them, some standing, others sitting down, all with arms folded.

It seems the further the photos go back in time, the students were rugby football players.

Some private boys' boarding school, maybe?

When did it morph into a special school?

It would be good to find out.

Another project...

I did find out... the information is on the web under Hopwell Hall Special Residential School...

~

Because the school was on open land, I never knew what borders meant, but I was soon to find out.

Little did I know we were right next to a girl's convent school run by nuns.

One day we were collecting apples from up a tree and the two boys I was with suddenly disappeared. I was just left up the tree with apples in my hand and, sure enough, when I looked to the ground, there was a woman dressed all in black bar a white collar.

She was middle-aged, plump and had a no-nonsense look on her face. She asked me to come down, which I did, and I followed her to my first time in a convent.

She led me through the corridors and into this big, brown room.

She sat me on a chair and she sat behind a large, brown table at the opposite end of the room and started to write something.

She did not look up once or speak to me the whole time.

Slowly, I began to take the room in. There was a large wooden cross behind her and the room seemed very still and quiet. After what seemed like a long time, she stood up, took me by the hand and led me back to our field, without a word spoken between us... and I kept the apples.

Jast a thaaght.

Why you talkin' like that?

It's not posh.

I'm tellin' Mami.

I'll say, *"Mami, yu see that Gloria Gaynor photocopy trouble? She talkin like she walking sideways."*

"Child, leeve Gloria alone. It's not her fault she straiten her hair."

AUTHORS NOTES ON 'JAST A THAAGHT'...

We see this side of Mami again, the protective maternal one, reaching out to a stranger, but a familiar one, a sister.

This sister, a grown woman, seems out of place as seen by the child.

Mami's caring – leave Gloria alone, it's not her fault.

You would have thought this inquisitive child would have followed Mami's words.

Whose fault is it, then?

If it's not her fault...

Whose fault is it then she straightens her hair?

The term fault suggests an issue unresolved.

The term or question, 'Whose fault is it, then?' suggests it needs to go somewhere... the blame is not hers.

It's imposed, copied?

Has identity been compromised beyond recognition?

Also, the child's directness to the sentence and how it was delivered.

The child obviously thinks the woman is off the tracks.

The statement, 'It's not posh'...

Does this suggest the child knows what posh is?

Let's look at the phrase...

She talkin like she walkin sideways.

Does this suggest her accent is so far-fetched it's almost unbearable?

Even with Mami to a degree I sense a slight ridicule within her statement...

She straiten her hair...

What a point to pick upon.

The phycological episodes of acceptance and how one deals with its sterile tentacles...

The woman is clearly showing signs of cultural identity crisis – CIC for short.

Maybe not just her, eh?

Is this woman a coconut?

Well, is she?

She straiten her hair and speak and walk sideways...

8 out of 10 people called her a coconut. One went on to say...

Well, she had it reel... why she change? Ain't no sista o mine.

Just because she straightened her hair?

It's more than this.

They go strange, like they're above you.

I seen it too much. Mi tell ar stay arf di chicken, stay arf di chicken. Is nung she ah peck e out...

Winston! Fetch mi a ginga beer plees. Mek we dun dis tesis...

Is juss straight hair...

Reel taalk.

Is juss bleech skin...

Reel taalk.

Is juss batti re shape...

Reel taalk.

Is juss a facial job...

Reel taalk.

Is there no place for the true essence to blossom?

Another statement on 'Jast a thaaght'...

It's not that I'm against her in any way, as I wear a wig at times.

Everyone must find their own ways of acceptance of themselves.

But really, I feel sorry for her.

44

She's making it worse for herself.

Her wording is slow and strange.

It's as if she's trying out each word for the first time in sentences. It's hard to listen to.

The first time I heard her speak I had to turn around to see where that voice sound came from.

Was the child alright?

A little traumatised maybe?

What an experience...

Dear Sista...

Sorry if I haven't been a good brother.

How is your neighbourhood treating you?

Did you know the warrior queens are present, as the battle rages?

It began a long time ago.

You didn't start it, but you sustained it, strengthened the cause, but these modern vibrator jabbin' jaspers take all the sparkle.

Well, I'm not having it.

Never...

Although they do a good twerk.

It's wrong... unclean, polluting the minds. It has to stop.

Any suggestions?

Dear Twerk...

Where are your origins?

I saw what you did to that man's senses.

It was stiff like a rod in seconds and you – yes, you – twerked him till he came, and in public...

'Im blown by you twerkers.

Was it the vicar that made you do it?

Or was it a doctor?

Or an uncle, maybe?

Someone made you twerk.

Well, you'll be twerkin' that ass in hell seeing it's a hell dance...

Trying to twerk hell's fire off your charcoaled ass for eternity.

Cuya...

Using your ass as a weapon.

You twerked them to death and smiled.

The hell dance claimed many and many more.

Needed to find out more, so child went to Mami for me to find out the origins of twerk...

Mamiiii.

Mami.

Mami comin'.

"Mami, weh di hell dance cum fram?"

"Fram hell... is hell it hail fram mi pikni."

"Is the Shitty hell, Mami? I seed them twerk in here."

"Dem will twerk pon street carna... mi pikni yu yiy wide, meki narro nung plees."

"Yes, Mami."

Common Newsflash

Burnt umber on the run... you thieving pigment you.

It's a long sentence, for sure.

Why did you do it?

It was only a spoonful of light ochre.

There's a party tonight. Burnt umber are not allowed in...

At Home

What was this urge?

I accepted that I didn't live at home, and was totally at ease with it, or so I thought. We had a special silent bond, which was more cosmic in outlook, as my mother came from a line of natural plants and roots healers.

When I would visit, the kitchen was as I remembered before leaving home, always filled with dangling roots of many sorts, boiling tonics and all sorts of super foods like seaweed juice. This was the mid-'70s. We had this alongside spiced carrot juice, beetroot coconut juice, soursop, red sorrel with ginger (this one was my favourite), crushed pineapple juice, and many more. So you see, before I left home I observed all of this as I spent time in the kitchen when Mother cooked, and I always just watched quietly.

Sometimes Mother would sing, or she was silent – no in between.

I would marvel at how Mother would just burst into song; you would really feel it with the smile.

Also, I remember how, when the ice cream van came around, I would go and get it. What was interesting was I always went with this medium-sized glass bowl which would be filled with pink ice cream which me and my brothers and sister would enjoy.

I fully did not hold my mother responsible for having to live with different families before going into care, because I saw she was powerless in the presence of certain men.

When his car pulled up, you would piss yourself, go and hide like a rat. I remember the police coming one night as my older brother climbed through the top window of the house to escape him.

When I was 5, he decided I was going to learn to spell PAUL... he stood over me with a heavy leather belt and waited for me to write it down. Of course, my little fingers were shaking and any attempt to spell came out wrong.

Down came the belt over and over until one time I looked at the door and saw my mother, looking helpless but worried; this is why I do not blame anyone.

Also, my dear older sister had different ideas about her brief time living with us.

She must have been 12.

I remember her a little; she wore a nightgown and not pyjamas.

Also she is 6 years older. She and my oldest brother left to go and live with their American father. My brother, he went into the American navy for a long time.

I recall we received postcards from around the world.

I don't remember him much but he did come over from America about 20 years ago.

The stepfather...

He did many, many things. I remember sleeping between the kitchen door and the outside door with no blanket.

Sometimes I would wake as dawn was coming (this was normal), then straight to Infants with no breakfast.

Other times I would sleep in the coal bunker; this was creepy.

I remember four things vividly:

1. Being put into the coal bunker and sitting on the coal in complete blackness.
2. The family climbing the steps to bed. Sometimes I would count some steps.
3. The sound when he put the wood across the coal bunker door so I couldn't get out.
4. The eerie sounds from the coal as it moved beneath me in a restricted, confined space; darkness engulfed me quickly.

This went on for a long time and was normal.

One day I remember sitting at the table and looking up.

Our eyes met, along with a big brown fist which connected with my right eye and sent me flying; my eye was closed for quite a while.

When I went to school one day...

I never went home again. I wasn't even relieved, as all was normal, or so I thought.

It must have been winter because I remember driving in a car with a couple who took me from the school.

I fell asleep in the car. When I awoke it was dark.

The first family were very kind, with two daughters my age. We shared the bunk bed in turns...

"Top or bottom, Paul?"

"Top please."

They were a warm couple who made me feel welcome, but something still wasn't right, even in this comfortable, secure home.

I'm not sure how long I was there; it must have been for a while as I did settle a little and can remember the woman more than the man.

In fact, although the man was kind, he had a firmness that frightened me a little and I wouldn't speak to him.

This could have been why I was moved – I felt unsettled around him.

Although they were Caucasian, I was not aware yet of colour.

The families were kind, but I was in another space – totally.

I remember their kindness the most though.

Back to the school...

One day when I was 12, I had the urge from somewhere to see Mum, so I walked away. It was late summer, getting dark, around 9.00 to 10.00 pm.

All I remember was walking through field after field, then sitting near some cows, then falling asleep. The cows were still there in the morning when I awoke.

I managed to get myself to a main road and then to the village, which I knew a little as sometimes we would go to the church there for a service. Someone recognised me alone and I was taken back to the school.

I remember the headmaster being really firm and upset.

This caused chaos, as his firmness triggered something. I went silent.

Later he asked me why I had run away.

I told him I wanted to see Mother. He told me that a lot of people, including the police, were looking for me, and that I was never to do this again.

[Home lingua – 'look at that']
Cude...

UNSEEN BOUNDARIES

It's not funny.

What you playin at?

Did you not consider the neighbours?

Did you?

One was enough, but 2...

2 in such a short space o' time.

Have yu gone completely out of your mind?

I can just hear them behind the curtains...

2 darkies in 1 month!

Who would of thought it?

Seems like butter don't melt in her mouth.

Well, we want her out of this shared house.

She's not staying here, bringing home all those monkeys morning, noon and night...

Good morning spectrum.

You're not that shitty green are yu?

No sir – ochre, of the lighter shade.

I'm a relative of mauve...

51

Listen to ochre of the lighter shade.
No sir, I'm a relative of mauve.
Mi juss buss out an laugh.
What a eediat ocha tun..

Is it that bad ochre that you're associating with, mauve?
Rather than the browns?
Are you in denial of the ochre range – and its full spectrum?
Have to be careful – the ochre spectrum can be quite dark.
That's why it's important to say ochre of the lighter shade,
and yellow comes to people's minds...

And the mauve connection?

Between me and you, I'm lighter than mauve.
But you know mauve...
Always telling people 'is distant cousins are royal purple.
Hence the mauve tone.

Yes, I know.
I've seen how mauve operates. He's a liar.
Always stirring things, saying...
Look at blackie, look what blackie doing.

But you know what, blackie?
What?
Mauve is jealous of you.
You, blackie, hold the mysteries in your pigmentation.
Retro knows this and will always be close.
Retro loves our frequency and mauve's jealous.

Mauve sounds like worn out cloth.

Pure distraction, when everyone knows mauve's been into insurance scandals since scandal was first used as a word.

Look how mauve lives.

He's in the pockets of burgundy for sure.

Oh, blackie, you'll never see all that gold you once beheld.

And who cares?

Lee Scratch Perry does, and me, and me, and me...

Back to school...

About a couple of years later, I had the urge again, and off I went.

It was the fields that did it, not me.

Something about moving in that vast open space...

Even now as I write I can still see a boy in uniform rambling through the equatorial fields, bushes and lanes...

I tried again to make progress to go visit Mother; this time I made my way to the bus stop.

Once on the bus, the driver said, "Where you going?"

"Home." It did not dawn on me I had not a penny and was semi in uniform, and he said something about this road being busy. "Go and sit down."

He drove a little further on, then stopped the bus and told me to go into a building to ask them.

As I looked at the building, I could see it was the church, who promptly took me back.

I was in trouble...

This time I knew I was in trouble.

I was told to go and have a wash, then a medical check, then I changed clothes.

By the time it came to eat I was not hungry as I was filled with fear. It suddenly dawned on me I had done this before and promised not to do it again, and here was I about to meet Mr Hooper and a few other staff.

Well, when I said I was not hungry, they insisted as I hadn't eaten for more than 24 hrs.

Mrs Gordon, who understood, really helped by talking to me about running away. She said when I go people are worried for me as they don't know where I am. I was 14 years of age.

I had toast and Horlicks, then it was time for the talk.

When I went into the office there were quite a few staff in there all sitting down; it seemed a bit crowded.

I was given a seat and promptly looked to the floor, and remained so until asked to leave.

I don't know what happened; I went vacant and couldn't focus fully on what was being said.

It was only when Mr Hooper asked me kindly to leave them to have a talk that I stood up and quickly left.

Looking back, I think they were worried that I had a taste for it and maybe a school closer to mother might help. I don't know.

But Mr Hooper did have a gentle talk with me a few days later.

GHETTO LIFE

When I started to go home for weekends it was good. I would play with my younger brother. Although he was 4 years younger, I would play with him a lot.

I tried to get a sense of the estate we lived on; it was okay, but rough.

Even in the local park you had to watch your back.

I remember going to the park with my older brother and an incident – it was one of many, but this one stayed vivid...

As soon as I climbed the steps to go down the slide, there was a fist waiting at the bottom.

"You effin' monkey," he laughed, showing his young crooked broken teeth.

These were the local indigenous white youths of the estate.

Some mixed, others didn't...

But I didn't understand race so when he said *effin monkey* it didn't make sense to me, just the fist.

He had obviously seen Tarzan and thought I was one of the extras gibbering around Tarzan with trembling rubber lips... no thank you...

I looked at his fist waiting for me when I slid down, but I didn't go down; I came back down the steps.

There was something that I cannot describe about going backwards down the slide steps – it didn't seem right.

It stayed with me even until today.

I know my brother was nearby, but bullies were always in the park.

This one in particular was a true bully – there was not much to him either, but he had a mouth on him and he was always making trouble.

When I went into care I didn't see the bully for many years. I had been away and had now come back as a young teenager.

One day, when I was about 17, I met the bully.

It was odd how we met, but we just did.

It was like we had a space and a time of our own to reconnect.

It was like...

Don't I know you from somewhere? As our eyes met, the past was refreshed and the bully was exposed.

Once this realisation took place, the term 'monkey' came to my mind and his fist waiting for me.

We both recalled it mentally then parted...

MY TUNE DAT

What other artist sang the song 'It's a Shame' by the Spinners?

Yes, you're right...

The late and great Alton Ellis.

And if you haven't heard...

Man tun down di blastid raidyo nuh man fi 10 minute, so mi cyan heer di cricket dem.

Yu know ow mi lov di soun ah dem dis time a day.

Ya.

Yes, mi sweet pum plum...

Yow weh yu meen pum plum?

Is wah kina nastiness ya chat?

Yu ah nyam it out too?

Is joke don't?

Tell me nuh, bwoi.

Mi feel fi tell Mami.

But Mami seh is so dem staiy.

Yu cyan tun plum ah cherry an daag goat.

Is so dem staiy.

*Nor Uncle Tickle, whom will say bwoi is heven me reech
pon ert.*

But I can tell that man over there waiting for his dog to
finish a shit...

Second thoughts, better not; they hold those shitty bags for
too long.

*But look, look who ah pass – a man in a green suit and
green brief case.*

He does look interesting, so I'll just ask him.

Scuse me, sir.

You look black British.

Do you mind answering a few questions?

Are you undercover?

Yes, I'm fully dressed.

I mean no, no...

Brother man, what a thing to say.

*Undercover – I get what you mean but I realise yu jokin
me right?*

The brother's face did not change; no smile came nor an indication to move forward in conversation.

As I was about to thank him and walk away, he spoke...

Brotha man speaks...

I'm a representative of the Shitty, shitty green.

The suit comes with the job.

I know what you're gonna say but I dissagree.

If man waan nyam owt – ha feem ting.

Not my ting but ah feem yu seet?

This is not my concern we too much eena peeple tings – let them be man.

If it nah trubble yu leff e...

Tek di advice an step man...

Yu heer dat, from a black British intelligent man working for the Shitty in shitty green...

Estate Ghetto – or Shitty – it's all the same in the concrete jungle run by hustlers.

The place is a hustle.

Why yu got me hustle?

Aint leff school yet, but I got a patch fo shor...

Familiar sound ain't money yu can eat.

This ere realiti... imposed upon me and shado.

Gatta break loose... with my own cashier.

The bad men, good men, musical men, quick-talking queens with heavy sway.

The younger guys my age were always aspiring to the older ones, who would reward them for being rude or being smart with their dialogue.

A pattern of lingua was changing all the time.

Some would be stable, others fade, but it was always fresh banter.

The songs were constant, alongside the fights.

Most wanted to be a DJ, *a toaster*, a reggae one at that, this side of the Shitty.

Sweet, recalling those musical days of sound systems.

Even in the gang groups you had all nationalities; even today they are mixed, but the media always portrays them as one bad race, mainly black.

What's that, I hear you say there – Charley Brown.

That's because most crimes are committed by them...

Can you say that again?

Yes, that's because most of the crime is committed by them...

And again...

What's this, then? Getting too hot for ya?

The facts... man.

Nobody wants to be around those gangs in society.

They won't go to school, they carry weapons and have a massive chip on their knees...

I tried to mix with a few of the guys on the estate, but it didn't work out as they knew of my school and I was referred to as Frankenstein or other demeaning names. Basically, you were the scapegoat, which I resented.

I'd get into a few scuffles with the other guys just for being there.

I couldn't believe how the hustle ran so smooth.

I'd say...

I'm out of the Shitty for a new shitty,

cos they all shitty.

Shitty rule.

A letter to Shitty...

Oh Shitty, there were a few queens that ah did like, Samantha being one of them...

Samantha went up to Clarence an' say,

"Where's Paul gone?"

"Gone back to that spastic school. Him and Jarvis go to the same school. Dem yout deh strange dread but Paul alright, a little strange but him alright."

"No, he's not alright. Why should he be alright? Is he locked up in that school? What kind of school is it anyway?"

"Neville said it's a school for kids no school wants to have in their school. He said some of the kids are deranged, mad. They got cells there with chains on the wall. It's weird but quite stayed [unchanged]."

~

There are always positive people who inspire the cause despite the oppression. This I have witnessed, and it strengthens you wholeheartedly. Society needs more role models, not just the bad ones.

I like variants of rap music as it is part of the culture. Now most cultures have rappers – see something?

JAZZ, REGGAE, BLUES

Reggae music is a part of me.

Likewise jazz, blues, folk, soul, classical music.

I heard it in the cosmic waters as my mother cooked and danced to it, and when I came out ska, mento, rock steady were staples... the varieties are endless.

Let's big-up all the early pioneers in this music.

When in my early 20s I really began to listen to the early Wailers and everything fell into place again.

I was spellbound by the mystic sounds and frequencies.

Even though they were trained singer vocalists, they sang in a strange harmonic structure with a distant, faraway sound, and not forgetting the lyrics were totally from outer space, foreboding cosmic consequences for the lack of respect of humanity.

Some of the songs, like Mr Brown's, would follow you around. You really saw the reality of the message, and, yes, they lived in the Shitty for many years.

In the early days, whenever they played, pandemonium broke out.

The world wasn't ready for them, although they had come.

Now that the original Wailers have all passed, firstly Nesta, then Peter and recently Jah B, now the phenomena really starts as they are in spirit, and what a mighty spirit they be.

I have heard many conversations about the Wailers versus the Beatles and who were the best.

For me, although I love the Beatles, as some songs they sung are a part of me now, the Wailers from the '60s – the original Wailers – do for me every time...

The smash hit from the '60s 'Simmer Down' is the start...

Back to the Shitty...

It didn't take long to realise growing up how the media can really screw up a community, and hence create a lack of trust.

You must remember, I was once a young KMT man growing up in these places – a melting pot to a degree, but also a cesspit.

I realise it is a harder life living this way.

For all people living here...

Something the mothers must have feared a lot when the young rude boys ventured out into the night and then school in the morning.

~

One reggae show I recall was the Chris Goldfinger show, starting at midnight on Radio One.

This was a bad-ass show, and the ratings for the show were phenomenal.

The show was one of the great wonders of the world, a show that fulfilled all your senses, leaving you super-charged. The jingles alone needed their own shows – especially the ones about Doris that one *keel de reel*.

Every interview with a reggae artist was not just educational but also inspiring.

This is why I took to it.

One thing I noticed that kept happening till I fully became aware of it was that most of the call-ins and big-ups were from people in prison – Lockdown: *grey, grey ship-out*.

At one time I thought he was broadcasting from prison itself.

A friend who teaches surfing asked me where he could listen to reggae on the radio and, after two attempts at the show, he found it too heavy, with all the prison big-ups.

This had me thinking – why so many people in prison?

Yaa mi juss waan big up k9
Juss ole down yu sentence mi bredda
What else can k9 do but 'ole it dung?
Is a big up all the same.

After drifting from the show, I went back for more big-ups and *Doris show gaan, Get ship out...*

...so people find their own ways to survive.

But you still have to pay the man for the hustle.

No pay = prison.

~

I recall a TV show from the '80s showing thieves, and I always prayed it wasn't a black face.

The build-up was terrible.

The presenter would talk about a serious crime worthy of TV. And you would gasp at the crime and then the description – this was more traumatic as your identity itself was at stake.

You closed your eyes tight waiting for the description, with incantations of *please don't be black, please don't be black.*

And then a regular, steady flow of black, male faces came upon the quiet British screens; not only that, but you thought that those ravaging monsters are on the loose, I suppose.

The situations made me very aware of my colour, but not identity...

This was something different.

But to the colour issue, I needed to see positive people, not criminals all the time.

I had now realised we were the minority, although I did not know what that word meant, but I was slowly, like a tranquilliser, realising I was in the wrong jungle.

Did this compensate for the police brutality?

My young mind was continually going through experiences that told me so.

Nor did I fully grasp slavery.

So I had to go directly to the source...

It is a medical issue now – not that kind of Medical, but certainly medical.

I know you're all thinking pot, ganja; no, that's not what I mean, although as we know 'tis the supreme doctor.

Cannot anyone see it's a medical issue, but not that medical. The view needs to be non-medical, not just medical.

But they on the big pharma conveyor belt, going round and around and around.

[Home lingua – 'look at this']
Cuya...

THE BALLAD OF THE CAGED

This cage 'as no shame
This pain 'as no pain
This wall in me 'as toppled me down
This wall in me as toppled me down...

This frequency is all over the world.

Every second of the day that ballad comes on the frequency,

Saying kin o' kin...

A flicker of light, a flicker of you.

But you don't.

You come with the jab to sedate the poor Negro into another state of no shame, no time – toxic frequency follows him.

He dribbles, staining 'is top.

His bottom lip hangs like bacon.

And he smells,

So high on his medication.

Like a child he fumbles with 'is fingers,

And like a pig in mud he mumbles some strange sounds.

Poor negro in mud – I'm on my way.

Me and Tarzan – or they won't let me in.

If I go on my own they'll think I'm one of the patients.

And when we arrive,

We shall sing, yes sing.

Sing through our souls so we are one again; even Tarzan knows this and is very sorry for making those Backbush Primi films of rubber-lipped Sambos always looking star struck.

Tarzan even transformed himself into a good luck ambassador for tree climbing.

Some things we just can't let go of...

~

And you, sister, you... mother priestess.

When you go mad everyone hides behind rocks.

Cos your spirit is crazy in this state – you cursing every single thing at the top of your voice, and your eyes remind me of Nina Simone.

I know you're not really mad, just trapped in a living spell.

But you did partake in it, dear Sadie...

We all do.

You had free reign.

What you did was your choice that brought you to this place; now open wide and take your medication.

You wouldn't joke with this stiff nurse.

Sadie takes the medication, her frail back is bent. Sadie wears a new hat today, pink and turquoise with yellow dots everywhere.

The brim of the hat covers her Nubian forehead.

Sadie, we will always love you, even though you prefer women – *je préfère la femme... pour la pudding...*

SADIE

Sadie was a slave to her desires
Born to hustle on smiling streets
Her brother was a vicar
Her mother a lady
Her father a mason.

Sadie shot a woman over a woman.

And Sadie went mad
Locked in the cage house now for the past 18 years
Now listen 'ere pussy-eatin' jasper mammal
I been there meself
I been there meself
I been there meself, and we be comin'
With peppermint candy and Anita Baker.

Yes, Anita Baker; we all been there, Sadie. Can't you see it? You's not alone.

I been *thare* myself, Sadie.

When I came upon you in that room with that bitch jasper between ya legs, entwined and growlin' to pleasures of the flesh.

Honestly, Sadie I nearly fell over.

But something made me stare...

What a pleasure you seem to have been having nyamin' each other out.

I stood there transfixed. It was so bad, Sadie.

Not you too. The fact that I just stared.

Sadie, I wish I hadn't of seen that kind of pleasure with mongrels.

I say mongrel cos I seen you in the Past with many, many exotic mixed race jaspers, all o 'em Amazonian with small teeth and heavy breasts.

Do you forgive me Sadie for these thoughts?

Sadie did not speak. Her face was that of Bakongo.

She had suddenly become a priestess and I had confessed to her, and the Azande breeze brushed her high centric cheek bones...

Oh well...

We on our way with your favourite frequency to help us all out...

Where did she go?

1997 INTERVIEW PRELUDE
– FEMALE GERMAN REPORTER

Highly, highly gifted, he tapped into something beyond money, making the work seem indescribable, uncategorised, an unusual refinement...

For him, going to the studio was at the shallow river, listening, looking, engaging with frequency...

Does he know he's gifted? How is it?

Do you feel gifted?

Well, I feel like a rock, a swing, a smile. All these gifts makes one feel gifted.

Do you mind being black?

[Why do you have to go and spoil the interview?]

Well, actually I don't mind, depending on... depending on... what country I'm in.

You mean you culture switch?

Yes, I do. When I'm in Russia I'm android and they fully embrace me.

When I'm in Cuba I'm not sure.

[Dear Cuba, do you like blacks, browns, whites, yellows or pinks or blues?

Cuba did not reply...]

One time I went to Guyana and was expected to be local.

When at a bar restaurant, I asked for a smoothie: oat milk and banana...

They looked at me strange.

Weh dat?

Banana and oat milk smoothie or shake...

Don't you know it?

Next I went to... yes, you guessed it, Ireland.

Now, let me tell you this...

You see that little, sleepy place on the map called Ireland?

One raas mighty lion dat place deh.

Ireland ha stretch out ha claim space...

PSYCHOLOGICAL MANIPULATION

A vivid memory I recall was a famous sportsman called Frank Bruno crying on TV, stating between the tears, "I'm not a coconut. I love my people."

This also showed the double oppression and the hatred shown to blacks from blacks, which is more coherent as some seek a level at any costs, fed up with the poverty served on a platter, with cyanide for dessert from the 4 corners of the globe...

There are 9 elements.

3 have been contaminated. The rest are cosmic.

INTERVIEW – BULL BAY, WEST INDIES, 1874

When did you move back to Bull Bay?

Well, it's been a while as it's continually tidal.

Is it how you imagined?

No it's not, the signal is faster than broadband.

Are you looking forward to going back into the future?

Yes and no.

What do you mean, yes and no?

What do I mean?...

Does this suggest time travel?

Yes and no...

MOTHER

My mother like most mothers has to work, to achieve many things in their lives.

The love is unconditional in most cases.

The life for the immigrant is written upon their faces...

Their foreheads want to go home but they can't...

It was only the cosmic Mayal side where Mother was truly free...

Leave the mystery alone...

FREE PORTLAND PORTAL

Well, the trees have sessions on how to behave on planet earth.

When I got there a fat woman was trying to lose weight to get back through the portal.

She'd been fasting for seven seconds, which in this place is literally eternal.

I felt she was pretending. She asked me in between mouthfuls of this green, sticky stuff that resembled baobab porridge, "Why have you come?"

I told her that the portal on the front said simulation world, so I thought to experience it...

Immediately I thought, this place is full of trickery.

Once the realisation seeped in there was no portal left, so I took the right...

71

This place was full of drugs of all kinds available to anyone – any age.

Also weapons, again of all kinds.

Where did these drugs and weapons come from?

My mother mentioned something about it in her home town in Jamaica in the mid-'70s.

This peaceful, idyllic place was suddenly filled with drugs and weapons.

The prostitutes were also protected by the same men.

The hustler came in all ages, sexes and colours.

When I was growing up in the late '80s the term hustler was highly respected.

If a man was a hustler he had money, and money in the Shitty is worth more than breath...

Shitty green ...

The green is dead. Babilan killed it, carbon copied it, put a patent number on it.

It's not my green, and guess what? I'm not telling Mami – she knows already cos she planted carrots and got large ones that smelled of metal...

~

You see, when you're born into something, you don't know anything else. This is why we have to be careful with children – don't fill them up too much, and they have to be able to converse and hold a level conversation, not just one-sided; in other words, not be brainwashed...

~

I saw a woman once beat up a man. It didn't look like he wanted to fight her, and couldn't. She was rough, and odd in a strange way as she smiled at most people and you felt like smiling back.

~

The hustler was always about and you could see the older ones teaching and ripping off the younger ones.

I recall people talking about the yardies in the '80s – but who really were the yardies?

Not just the name, but the organisation behind them, as they had access to a lot of arms / air tickets / weapons / cars / Class A drugs, and moved easily around the world...

I don't accept they were a bunch of Jamaican rude boys...

But look at the sensationalism around them: the films, books, T-shirts, etcetera.

I needed to see it to show how people hide behind identities to commit crimes.

Still in the Shitty...

It wasn't all harsh. I met some sound people, many good people, including my mother's few friends on the estate.

It was a close-knit ghetto.

Most people knew someone you knew and this is how it was.

The young men were just being themselves, but I preferred the musicians to hang out with.

I recall a musician called Wesley, a young guy about 17, very mellow even then, who carried a guitar.

He would jam on the estate and sing folk songs. He was like a hippy as he did not wear fashion, just extra-long, woolly jumpers, plimsolls and thin trousers.

He totally was not into fashion and stood out.

So there was individuality from the start.

After leaving school I saw him less as he had a job and was at college doing music.

Even then the term college seemed a foreign tongue word.

It seemed such an important place that I never considered the school I came from...

~

Even before going into care, my mother was always working. I hardly saw her sit down, which had me wondering later on in life, is it all about work?

What about stillness...

Stillness was stolen from the masses and sold back to them as spirituality.

And guess what?

I'm telling Mami. I'll say, "Mami, how can people charge for spirituality?"

This time Mami laughed so loud, I thought she was going to burst. When eventually Mami stopped laughing and composed *she self, she start laugh agen...*

I say, *"Mami, dis no joke."*

Mami laughed and said – *"Is di biggest joke yet..."*

Back to school...

We used to have story time with Mrs Gordon – Bible stories. We would all sit on the floor around her and she would read. 'Jonah and the Whale' I remember most.

From her low stool she would read for a long time as our imaginations would take in these tales of woe...

Mrs Gordon...

I remember Mrs Gordon as an ample woman.

Plump.

With big hair.

She wore those two-piece lady suits, not trousers.

What I remember about her was her warmth.

She had a fine, full smile that made you laugh or smile back, no matter what.

In a sense, she was a true matron as you could relax with her any time, no matter what, and we needed maternal care of a sorts.

She also did cooking with us alongside the dinner ladies.

The dinner ladies...

When I think back now, these dinner ladies would have had to travel far to get to work.

Even the nearest bus stop was a long way off, then the long walk up the drive.

They were always happy and quite loud sometimes.

I think I liked them the most.

They talked a lot and gave us samples of food or nibbles.

This was the '70s – very laid back.

~

A lot happened at this school set in the rolling hills of Derbyshire. It was a place to contemplate nature as we played whilst learning.

Back to the Imbecile...

When I was informed by my mother that a test on me at the age of 7 revealed I had the IQ of a 2-year-old, this came as a shock to me as I tried to figure it all out.

Where did this come from?

Was I abnormal?

A retard?

An imbecile, as they clearly stated?

But why?

Who came to this conclusion, as it has left me, even with all my skills, still perplexed and left out... it's not something you can say 'it's okay' to...

I grew up, saw the same things, so even today I don't go to the doctors much.

My take on the Follywood...

Liberation on the plastic screen.

Welcome to Follywood.

It is a reality that has been played out for as long as the TV has been around.

Have you noticed we can get...

Our freedom

Our justice

Our liberty

Our unity, only on the screen.

Only on the Follywood blockbuster will you find our true redemption...

Pause...

And people flock to it, shedding tears at the injustices played out by carbon copy, black, superstar actors making millions, but nothing changes for the ghetto youth – or the elderly.

It's just money for the big producers and actors.

When you see them at the Oscars, all black and shiny like new ebony sculpture, you have to laugh, and at the same time cry.

What's the point of watching yourself being oppressed in film?

It just adds to more anguish.

There is nothing to gain in drama school or acting if nothing changes in the community, which it clearly hasn't, but every year there is a new sensation, a new actor or actress to play out a new perspective of the oppressive eras...

I sound like a film critic.

At the same time, films like 'Porgy and Bess' stir a deep steady emotion where memory meets candy via operatic cosmic expansion...

The faces of the mamas makes ya jess wanna go en dry cry...

It's all the same in Sabo Land.

Not that I dismiss the message...

We know about the suffering.

Making film after film after film will keep it on the screen and on people's minds but, if you live it daily, that's channel switching...

Unless seeing film after film of oppression finally clicks and the whole B Movie becomes real.

Yes, you recall the anguish as it's in a creative format but it's entertainment... for you to enjoy or not.

But what about Melvin van Peebles' 'Badass Sweetback' epic film?

Didn't that expose the blaxploitation film industry?

Yo bro were yu goin?

I ain't finish yet.

But the late Gill Scott-Heron was accurate...

Why wasn't our universal past being accepted?

The ancient artefacts add to this; it's evident in the features and great temples that we had greatness, and still do.

This is the level I arrived at after realising my whole history was a lie.

Again, Gill Scott-Heron in one of his many classic griot schoolings...

The term 'His story, not mine': this is his story, not mine.

It's like another identity.

You see, I come from an ancient space.

Our great artefacts and pyramids state this.

And a lot of the obstacles are of a race issue. This way it's a hindrance to progress or have any self-belief...

...of oneself and my race. It's all been altered to deny my epic past.

But again the mainstream archaeologists would try and have us think differently...

Denying our epic global past, which today is so evident.

All our great past being interpreted by other people, who don't have our knowledge or our interests at hand?

When did this happen?

THE IMBECILE BADGE

I vaguely remember the test, being asked to build some blocks and count numbers and other little logical actions.

I thought I did okay as I was 7 at the time.

I can remember going with my mother to this place, like a day centre with quite wide rooms, bright lights, etcetera.

I never asked what diagnosis I had.

But I knew something was not right.

It would take time to see how the cuckoo knows no roost...

So I had a label put on me, and yet they would not tell me, just that I am an imbecile.

Back to school...

The season I remember most was when winter came.

It was our job to clear the snow off the road leading to the hall with fields on either side. It would take most of the morning to achieve this task but we enjoyed it once we got going.

Sledging was also fun. This would go on straight through winter, so we really lived the outdoor life. We didn't have much flu or colds as we were living fresh.

I remember looking out of the dormitory windows at night and seeing distant bright lights. This must have been Derby.

But the hall building was imposing as you looked down on everything from this view.

The hills at night with the snow looked like upside down, oversized shapes merging. The dip was filled with snow, and the contours and shapes would change in spring, summer, and autumn. I began to grasp the rhythm of elements...

CHRISTMAS

Christmas was pure fun. We would all have lunch in the main hall, which was decorated, and then we would eat as much as we could.

Also the girls from the convent next door would come over for a disco.

The girls...

At 14/15/16, I had no interest in girls and at one time someone suggested I was gay...

Well, that's not true either. It took its time, that's all. I did have a long-standing first relationship and, would you believe it, with a teenager from a convent school. We were tight, then for three years later.

You could say that was the first attraction and eventually the experience.

Back to school...

We danced and laughed with the girls for a while, then maybe we would go outside in the snow.

Most were waiting for Santa and their presents.

Even today, after five years of presents, I cannot recall any of the presents.

We would sing carol songs in the school and village, wrapped up in warm jumpers and coats.

In winter we wore long trousers.

We really enjoyed the atmosphere of it all.

I remember when we had to queue to see Santa in the long, brown hall lit up with Christmas lights and receive our present.

Prior to all the previous visits, this one was to be the last. Our eyes met for a brief moment as I was 15 and thought I recognised those eyes as Mr Danes', but it was just a personal thought that stayed with me.

It would be good to find out who our Santa was for those five years.

The 'Generique' Christmas

Every child has a Christmas memory.

Mine was sealed by Miles Davis' track 'Generique'...

Because of the landscape, the fragility of the moment and the vast space between...

My situation had all the settings for this track, just like the poem 'The Stone' written in 2007.

It was Christmas and I was going home for the holiday, because it was a residential school in the middle of nowhere, plus it was a full Christmas winter scene by the time we arrived at the town.

It was dark, and my family had moved address and I had to find the new house.

I recall being 14, arched low in the snowfall, trying to find this address given to me by the school for how to get home.

I did eventually find the new house on the estate.

But the welcome I received was not good.

I was the visitor to some, and they made it plain.

But my mother was always on a level, so the foundation was okay.

CHURCH

At home, before going into care, I remember going to church every Sunday.

We had to polish our shoes at home and look smart.

We, the children, sat at the back, the parents at the front.

It was a crazy scene when I look back now.

It's nothing like the English church services.

At these services you would see women collapsing in spirit, people speaking in a frenzy and the preacher condemning all the imminent world troubles on abiding with sin.

You know, when I was listening to that documentary on the radio about women going abroad to get a bigger bottom and one operation went wrong, the first thing I thought of was the church...

Hundreds of mainly black women go abroad.

Why are so many black women having the shape of their body changed – breasts, buttocks, facials?

Back to school...

THE SUMMER

Summer was beautiful and full of outdoor activity with fruits, gardening, cooking and visiting places.

The sun shone bright and hot and I remember the yellow-green T-shirts we could wear or the white shirts.

The crickets were the loudest of all the insects and I was fascinated by their lime green armour.

I got stung by a bumble bee as I held it gently in my hand. It wasn't the pain, it was the disbelief that I had been stung. I did not tell matron although my palm seemed a bit swollen, but I never picked up a bee again.

The summer evenings were long and warm, sometimes going to bed with sunshine coming through the curtains.

ADVENTURE

Some of us would get into the van with a teacher who would drive us to a location.

I remember once going to a theme park and being lost for a while. It was huge, with lots of different things to see and do.

One time we went all the way to Scotland and stayed in a youth hostel. On the menu that first night was onion soup. Now, from the look and the smell, we should have left it alone, but it seemed that was all that was on the menu. It didn't take long for our little stomachs to vomit it all out – even now I can see about eight of us in the toilet vomiting this ancient Scottish broth called onion soup.

Putting that aside, the mountains were incredible.

I clearly remember taking a turn high up and suddenly not hearing a thing.

The teachers wondered where I'd gone...

Not far, but the wind took sound away.

A lot of arrangements must have been prepared for this trip and I am truly grateful for whoever made it happen.

I remember going for bush walks in the summer, on my own or with a friend. We would be away for a few hours, just roaming and having fun in the fields as part of play time, and routines all seemed to merge into one...

We would also do planting in the spring and picking in the summer, autumn and winter.

The tomatoes were my favourites as we picked and ate them fresh. They were always big and juicy due to Mr Gordon's knowledge of the earth, which we all took a keen interest in.

Thinking back now, Mr Gordon was like a pioneer man, a man from the hills, with a bushy beard and a short-brimmed hat. He knew a lot about outdoor building activities, also looking after poultry and other projects.

I stuck close to Mr Gordon as well...

He was funny, if I remember, but a very interesting character. One day he removed his pipe from his mouth and blew into an handkerchief; all the smoke slowly came through and left a dirty brown stain.

He explained this is what you get from smoking, which didn't make any sense to us.

A kid asked if he could have a go. No one spoke but quietly they were laughing.

Back to the farmyard...

We had an orchard, and kept some poultry: geese, chickens, ducks, and a domestic fox called Vicky who we would feed. Mr Gordon had made an underground bunker and the fox would come for the feed then promptly disappear. That's what I remember; she never stuck around like dogs.

Also, the redcoats would randomly charge through the grounds. One time I was just leaving somewhere when I heard the hounds and thundering feet. I stood stock still and then they came; it seemed like hundreds of them. Following were the redcoats on horseback charging through. I was 12 and stood stock still. One old man waved at me, then I was gone.

Even though we had our own space we still mixed a lot.

I can clearly recall discussions or listening to others speak.

There was a range of vocal expression and wording I noticed.

Some spoke quietly all the time, some were loud all the time, some were emotional and some frustrated.

It wasn't limited words, it was how the conversations would be. Even jokes would be odd, but we would laugh all the same, no longer autistic...

In the school where we lived most of the students were on the autism spectrum.

As I look back now at the behavioural patterns and actions and reactions, it was so obvious. I don't see this behaviour in people much not on this autism spectrum.

What is autism?

I don't know...

From a young child I did not say much and focused a lot. That didn't concern anyone.

...Constantly in another space and time.

I had no interest in anything and was vacant a lot.

But if I was given, for example, a small transistor radio, that would be it. I found a world in the wiring and battery of the radio – this was my new world.

I treated it like a teddy and took it everywhere.

Not necessarily listening to it, but studying its functions.

I would thrive on the beep station on short wave.

The sounds were quite soothing.

One of those frequencies I liked, and still listen to them today, but not on that scale like then I was 10.

One Christmas, my older brother and cousin, two bullies, broke my transistor intentionally.

All hell broke loose once they realised what they had done as I could not be pacified at any cost and avoided them completely.

My older brother never really understood my differences but merely tolerated me by bullying me and denying my mannerisms as if I was someone visiting.

But overall he is a good brother.

This could have been another reason why I had to do that test aged 7...

I saw this same behaviour in our school and when I began to work with special needs students of all ages.

I never felt so relaxed as around special needs people, as I identify with it. I can only see things from certain ways, and that's it.

You can repeat it over and over and even when it goes in it is interpreted differently...

CARPENTRY

Carpentry was what I enjoyed most at school. The teacher and some of the other students made furniture a lot so got to know where everything was.

No machines, all by hand.

But it was still under the instruction of the teacher.

We had about four lessons per week in carpentry, as other students were being taught.

Looking back now, Mr Walters taught in a basic, structured and quiet way.

When he talked, it was calming, like how a friend, mother or father could be.

He would help mend the plane when a knot got caught in it.

He couldn't get me out of there.

We, I, thrived on these projects as Mr Walters was good at his work on a humane level.

Mr Walters was the main inspiration for me in the whole time I was at the school.

~

Another strong memory I have is of Mr Slinksy.

A short, stout, powerful man with no teeth and longish white hair, he resembled an ogre, a real one.

He was in charge of heating the school with coal.

One day he called me over to the boiler room to look at the furnace.

We walked down some steps and I sat on one of the steps as he proceeded to the furnace.

87

He took his top off and started to stoke the furnace with a long metal rod with an open flat end. I was transfixed. The heat from where I sat was quite warm but he was right in front of the furnace. He suddenly turned around and had this frenzied look on his face with a wild toothless grin.

He seemed to be part of the fire. I really took it in, then left. He was a very good man, always smiling, with an unusual warm presence...

We were an odd bunch, all mixed together. One friend had small breasts, another would continually read out numbers; he was called Jeffery. I remember him as quite slim, thin-faced with longish black, curly hair. Looking back now, he could have been Irish.

One would be mapping out the constellation, always pointing to the sky and talking about cloud formations and weather. I remember him but not his name. He would also keep passing out with nose bleeds all the time. Some were short, very fat, deformed, silent, loud. Some rocked back and forth. One randomly started banging his forehead against the wall; he was called the woodpecker. Others I am not sure of, but we had each other.

Looking back now, we were a mixture of races.

A young, tall man with an afro called Noel used to be a former pupil and I remember him just like the other staff.

It wasn't like, 'Yo brotha Noel, gimme five.'

Because I remember talking to him, but not about race...

We would have to deal with it soon...

Sometimes I wonder what he was thinking about what we were going through, what he had been through – he seemed well and together, very inspiring if I remember. He must have been a very popular pupil.

He was always standing up when I saw him and he was quite tall.

I do remember looking at him, taking him in.

But that's it.

There was a Spanish Mexican.

Indian African, mixed race, the KMT boys, of which I was one.

The other KMT boy came from the same estate as me, so I recognised him.

He was very tall for his age but didn't talk much.

He would stammer and get frustrated.

I liked him a lot and we were friends. Even after school had finished I would see him around.

He did not mix much.

Looking back now, Noel was always staring. Even now I can see him stare like a statue, still like one too.

Noel stared at a black boy growing up in a residential special school.

His height gave him away.

~

Dear Shilluk King, brother Noel, I come to you with important news...

Please consider it before you reply.

Now, I remember you staring at me a lot back then in the early '80s...

Truth is I didn't have a clue why you stared so much.

It was when the faggot chapter came up that I suddenly realised.

Were you shafted?

Please forgive my forwardness, it's just an enquiry of sorts.

I think you were and you thought I was. Well, you're wrong, and you're not my Shilluk King no more, and guess what?

I'm telling Mami.

I'll say, "Mami, that darki with spider legs kept looking at me strange at school. He would just stare. I think he was a prostitute."

And. Mami will say,

"Child, leave Noel alone. No body shaft him, but him experiment wid di bwoi dem."

"So Noel going to hell, Mami?"

"Yes, he going to hell for staring at vulnerable children."

"An di dinner ladies?"

"Well, some of the food I wouldn't give you, but *dem grow you so dem good.*"

"What about any naughty teachers?"

"Dem gaan hell already…"

~

And this is the point…

It's hard to try and fit into mainstream society.

Why?

 The approach from the start was somehow set differently; adding race and colour is quite complex.

We have our own unique visuals and harmony.

Something evident in our expression.

And I think we did the best we could and were in our own space and could just be.

Today somehow the authorities are saying I don't have anything and I will have to go on a waiting list to have that test again...

That's race for you.

~

Just recently on the radio a business woman came on Radio 4 stating, "I have just had my autism test and I have autism..."

The presenter asked, "How does this affect your business?"

The lady states, "I see things from a different perspective."

On hearing this interview and being told that I have to do the test again I felt at odds with it all...

Because of race and economics my status is decided, put on hold by people who always seem to miss the main factors...

Having to go and have a test to see if I have autism won't change anything.

It won't give me peace of mind, as I have had to find ways to adapt in society to my best abilities and also with help from friends, as in a way I live outside the system, but within, if this makes sense...

Brief trip home...

I remember going home for a while and going back with a broken wrist and lower arm which was in plaster for three months. When I got off the bus I recall the headmaster saying to some people as I walked past, "This is what happens when we send them home." I knew he was talking about me as he was looking at me when he said the remark.

It was an accident by my older brother who plays rough and didn't realise his own strength as he flung me in the air and landed on me. All we heard was this crisp crack and I leapt into the air.

But what was more interesting was how quick my wrist fingers and arm swelled up like a balloon, then I was rushed off to hospital.

I was put to sleep then awoke with this big plaster of Paris cast that was near to the shoulder. It was bent and in a loose bandage.

For the next three months there was no making the bed, tying shoes, putting a shirt on. It was all odd but very relaxed as the staff were like parents and I enjoyed their company.

FARMYARD

We had routines like feeding the fowls and preparing the feeds for the chicken, geese, and ducks. The feeds were from broken shells. We made them on a large spiral grinder which could have been used for mincing meat. As you filled up the top then turned the handle the shells would go down in a spiral and get crushed then were mixed with corn breadcrumbs and water then used as poultry food.

The farmyard area was at the side and going on to the back of the large building.

We had a long shed attached to it where we made things for the farm or stored things.

On the farm there were lots of buckets, I remember.

Wood, tools, and a large clump of cedars which gave off a nice fragrance in summer.

Also, a local farmer, Mr Clifford, would come over on a tractor trailer to deliver some straw and other goodies, like spicy apple pies from his wife's kitchen.

Sometimes Dora came with him, who told some of us that the apples were good for growing and seeding.

I would walk to the scattered hamlets and see the people living there who knew of our school, going into some of these unusual dwellings, made mostly of a hard sandstone, maybe grit stone?

The lanes to them closed in on you, with wild blackthorn and hazel fighting for space.

There are a lot of sayings in Derbyshire about blackthorn.

One goes like this:

Plant in spring

...avoid the wing.

~

Mr Clifford was quick with his eyes.

He scanned everything.

I was fascinated by his abstract qualities.

His rope round his waist.

His large hands on a short man.

Fixing his eyes on things only he could see.

He had a round face with a warm smile and seemed to be weatherproof.

He had this strong Derbyshire lilt to his tongue –

Aiyupp yung uns.

Helps mi tek this yaaire fudda tat barn yaaire.

We would laugh, not in a rude way, just because of the way he said it with no smile, but the words would escape from the side of his lips.

When we tried talking like that it would all fall apart.

Looking back, he is no different to some of the Devon bush farmers today. They have even got the same clothes on, 30 years later – rope for a belt.

I enjoy gardening. Even right up till recently I was gardening to help pay workshop bills, etcetera.

As a child, like most children, we played with mud.

I found mud to be an interesting material...

I recall collecting different colours and making patterns on the floor with the coloured mud. Even in the classroom I would bring mud inside and make little animals and marble shapes.

~

Because I enjoyed the outside, we went running with a sports teacher, Mr Alan – long distances through the fields and lanes.

In Derbyshire, fields equal bulls. Large ones, as we found out one day. We just leapt over the stye in time as the bull came screeching to an angry stop, making a sound I can only describe as tumbling boulders.

But it was running that I thrived on too, alongside carpentry.

I can clearly see about ten of us going on a cross-country run where we would run for miles.

Some of the guys stayed with the teacher at the front.

I always stayed at the back, taking it all in at a short distance back.

Maybe it was just the peace of running alone.

This soon changed as we were entered for competitions. I was 100 sprint, 400 long distance sprint, and hop, skip and jump.

These ones I thrived on. Oddly, I did like football but was crazy for rugby which we didn't play much, but I did prefer rugby.

We were all odd shapes so it was our kind of rugby, which seemed to work.

~

I enjoyed carpentry with Mr Foster and Morris dancing with Mr Shaw.

Mr Shaw had a traditional wooden Morris Minor car. He looked like John Peel a little, with a neat, black beard and tweed jacket. He taught us how to do basic Morris dancing steps.

Mr Shaw was a proper folk man as he always had these strange instruments and would patiently get us to hold them and try and play them.

But it was the Morris dancing where he truly came alive.

He had pipes, accordions and tabors, all in the middle of the room, and we would put on the Morris shoes and learn the basic steps.

I thrived on this and kept going to this lesson for as long as I can remember.

What I remember about Mr Shaw was the way he unloaded his car, carrying all those instruments into the hall.

Master carpenter...

Mr Foster, a very quiet, gentle man who always stayed on the same level.

He would have been around 65 to 70 and always wore a brown carpenter's coat. He had a thin, kind face and thin, white hair. I thoroughly enjoyed those moments as I spent a lot of time learning from him.

A lot of the furniture we made was displayed in the main hall, then I'm not sure what happened to them.

We made our own furniture, separately, not together.

We made tables and stools, a few cupboards, but tables were number one.

It was such a calming environment. I wanted to be there all the time.

I fully appreciated his calming temperament.

One good memory I have was when I was 14 and made a table for my mum. We drove it to her house, presented it, then we left. When I went to visit, that was the main table in the kitchen.

I only cried because I did not want to.

I only looked because the sound was familiar.

I only spoke to say goodbye...

WANDERER

Leaving the school is when I tried to grasp reality. For the next 30 years I became a kind of wanderer as I could not read and write so avoided anything that involved paper-filling, signing, meetings, etcetera.

The few times I did sign anything they just rubbed it out or ripped up the form, so I avoided this at all costs, but how long would this go on for? I needed to do something but was lost a little...

I did not know what to do. On the estate where my mother lived I was deemed stupid Frankenstein. They knew the school I had attended so I was bullied and forced to do things and got picked on when I said no and told them to leave me alone.

I resented being around them – not all of them, just the ones who were full of anger and hate, and there were plenty of them...

It was rough. Truly, I slept rough for a long time, but not many people knew as I did not sit on the streets and beg but just found a quiet place and went to sleep.

Some of the places were bin shoots on estates. They seemed to be warm so I slept there often.

One night a policeman came, looked at me and left. He didn't bother me.

This was normal, but also I hated it as I knew it was not right. It was too close to my delicate childhood.

Had I slipped through the net again?

IN BETWEEN THE LINES, 1989

Who agrees with the fine past, raise their left arm.

I wasn't surprised to see the full stadium raising their left arm...

And chocolate cookies?

Both hands went up, even gun salutes. Someone shouted, "They have the power."

What power?

They are important men and women. Read your books and see.

What book?

Any book you choose...

~

The Cayman Islands, off they went.

On the beach one day an old lady selling coconut water stopped nearby and took a rest.

They started chatting about the island, and the lady literally vanished in front of them.

They went back to their hotel room and never mentioned it again.

~

What black problem needs solving now?

Can't we solve mauve problems?

Mauve carried a gun, liked sci-fi.

Mauve had the gun for 27 years, a toy gun but a gun all the same...

Kin...

Is it you, sweet you?

It's copper black.

Are you Martian?

How did you guess...

I'm telling Mami...

About copper black being a Martian.

Mami, I callin'.

Mami.

Mami comin'.

"Mami, I met a Martian today – copper black," and Mami says,

"Is you cousin dat..."

98

~

You see, as an elemental worker, my interests are the unseen.

The things that make the unseen manifest happen on an elemental level.

~

Blackie, now listen here blackie, you need to buy a rocket; we have a mission.

That's why we got this rocket. We're sending you 4 yards away to find a new civilisation, and don't come back till you do...

Mami, Mami, is there another term for blackie?

Am I black?

If so I'm washing it off.

I'll scrub till it's all gone.

Won't I?

Yes, you will, you idiot...

NOTES FROM RUNAWAY COVE 2004

I came to this island to experience the people's way of being as these are unique ways to exist and ways of expression that will some day lead the world in cultural phenomena.

What do you mean by cultural phenomena?

What do I mean?

Back to Wanderer...
Although I was free I did not know it as I was still tangled up in who and what I was doing then...

99

Opportunities are always present no matter what situation you are in and because of my rural rearing people picked up on it and tried to help me, but by this time I was quite lost, confused and angry because I didn't fit into anything.

The adolescence years for every teenager are not easy – let's leave it there...

~

As I grew into a young man I had strong compassion for humanity. I loved humanity, because I was slowly realising that those who had helped put me on this road were complete strangers.

I stayed with many families, as I had done before going into the special school permanently.

~

I think earlier I mentioned natural phenomena...

Well, I didn't know the name of it, but I experienced a lot of it, and still do.

It has become normal.

On one occasion, when I was 17 and it was a bad storm, there was a strong warmth with me, which was odd, but I was grateful, although I did not understand how these things worked, but I did not forget it... this natural phenomena.

As I travelled around the country I ended up in Dorchester at about 7.00 p.m. in the evening with no particular place to go. I was told to get off the streets as a bad snow storm was coming.

I did not know where to go so I stayed in a hidden doorway curled up.

Then the snow started. It was howling and windy.

The snow was on my knees.

Then something happened.

I can only describe it as double glazing.

It became silent.

I couldn't hear anything.

The snow was sliding down, like on glass.

But I was warm.

I tried to take it in fully and the next thing I knew it was morning and I got up and moved on to Weymouth.

It was a nice coastal beach area.

The first time I was seeing the sea...

~

So I realised from all these things growing up that I have always experienced natural phenomena...

I could write a complete book on the natural phenomena I have experienced, and the visions also, as some of the visions came in seven-year cycles.

And although I had a strong love for humanity, this was changing. As much as I tried to hold on to it, I saw and experienced the full hypocrisy of humanity, not that I am not this myself at times but I could see a larger scale in society which caused a lot of problems..

Today 2000...

I am told that I am a gifted sculptor, ceramicist, having won awards for this research as an amateur mineralogist, all learnt. I also like playing the harp when I can.

All is slow and learned.

All these gifts that I have been given clearly show I am not an imbecile.

SOCIETY

Once realising I was allotted into the black box, all hell broke loose, as from my history I had not comprehended it was a huge experience, since I had been protected, and suddenly I felt I had to behave and act in a certain way...

1980 WANDERER

I missed the rural seasons already.

All expectations didn't exist.

I lived on Mars bars, crisps, R. Whites lemonade – '80s style...

9 FREQUENCIES

The nine frequencies of elemental sound.

A riddle...

Silver before

Gold after...

A QUOTE

James Brown quote...

James Brown said, "They kick you and you can't even say ouch."

Back to Wanderer...

Suddenly life was throwing dark matter at me and I did not know how to handle it, so I retreated back to the bush...

The countryside where I excelled and allowed the true me to come out, like when I do a sculpture – Mr Foster's inspiration is right by my side, smiling gently. Maybe he knew all along.

You see, in the school where I was raised, colour and race was not known. We were too young. Yes, there were different colours, but it was natural, no one stood out as different.

So when I was 18, yes 18, I had an experience that told me I was BLACK, whatever that meant...

This big, black thing I was expected to carry with sorrow and shame lingered for a while until I realised we had toilet paper too...

THE TIC FACTOR

I had gone to stay with my mother for a while and mixed with the local youth on the estate. It was a complete pecking order. You had to be careful all of the time.

Someone always wanted to test you – fight you – from nowhere or nothing you would be confronted to fight, which I never did, but I did get into a few scrapes.

You would constantly hear gossip about who's been arrested, who's just got bail, who's been sent to prison. All this seemed natural, but deep down I hated it totally.

I felt the hopeless weight of living in the Shitty – it is a complete no-no breeding ground of hate and loss. Yes, there are a few good moments to be had, but in reality again the term cesspit comes to mind.

For example, if I got stopped for mistaken identity I would be taken to the station and the officer would do a TIC on you, adding further crimes to be taken into consideration.

You felt the pressure of the police on you.

And I clearly remember saying yes to 23 TICs that I never did because of the way he spoke to me.

He had a patronising intimidation to his voice like we were buddies but he was in charge.

This TIC became normal. You would say yes and straight away he would bring out a file and add another 30 petty charges which the judge had to consider. I must have confessed to hundreds of TICs and yet I did not do one of them. I would really like to see my signatures on all those charges as I could not read and write yet.

I was on this dark merry-go-round till I left the Shitty. Even at that young age I had to leave.

This dark merry-go-round.

Why you spin me so.

And so?

There was this urge bursting that I could not contain.

One evening I clearly remember standing on a hill and thinking, tomorrow I'm out...

And sure enough the next day I walked away with not a penny, just started walking.

~

This preying on young, vulnerable men.

Sure, there are rude boys to be had, but don't all races have rude boys?

So what is this law that allows this to happen?

And what of justice?

It was all quick, in a systematic way. You had no chance to grasp any of it, as you knew what little freedom you had was at stake.

And yet I still could not see clearly why we were being constantly hassled most of the time, even back then.

There was a clear divide between them and us that they had created to make money out of the oppressions – this was obvious.

But what I remember most was the slackness, the lack of trust, as everyone was hustling from each other – the poor robbing the poor.

What would Robin Hood think of that?

~

And all this before I could sit down and properly appreciate Oscar Peterson!

As a child, I had seen and heard jazz but didn't know it as jazz, just music with space in it.

My mother had some old jazz albums. Ben Webster was one.

TURBULENCE

A social worker got me a room in a house and there I tried to settle down.

One time, when I was asked to attend a Job Seeker's interview, a man came into the room and put a white box on the table with documents in it.

He started talking to me about learning a skill, but I recognised my name on the box – bold black letters on the white box.

I could recognise my name, but writing it down was another story.

As I looked at my elusive name, there was a word underneath it in bold, black letters too.

As he spoke to me about jobs, I was more interested in the letters or words beneath my name as I knew they were linked in some way and I am inquisitive, even when I don't understand.

I remember trying to say mentally beneath my breath I.m.b.e Imbe but the last few letters Cile I was lost with.

Although I could see them, I could not put the words together.

When the man noticed how transfixed I was with the word on the box, he turned it around.

I did not hear one single word of what he said about training. That word, each letter, seemed to be printed on my psyche.

There the letters stayed and 30 years later I turned on the computer and put in the remaining letters.

What came back at me I was not surprised by.

Just saddened by it all... Imbecile.

This was when I was 18 and trying to find my way in the world, not knowing yet the complete discrimination I would encounter most of the time in all aspects, not just from whites but from all nationalities as I soon realised there was more racism towards people of colour from people of colour than from whites. This is a fundamental point I picked up on in the '80s, as I experienced a lot of bad vibes and comments from within the larger spectrum of the black nations' communities and individuals, and the list goes on...

The late and great Joseph Hill of the band Culture sang a song – 'Humble African'...

This word Africa was now following me around like a second skin.

Shoo shoo, go away Africa. Shoo – shoo. I chased Africa away, but Africa followed, even ridiculed me.

Let's see how this one copes with the realisation of his epic history and culture.

It was hard. I had not even at that time understood political parties, freedom fighters.

Countries, class, you just existed in your own Shitty where that culture was, that was it.

Even though some of the viewpoints you did disagree with, you held your tongue.

For example, defending gays is a complete no, no...

The culture is strong in the Shitty.

Make no mistake about that.

I would never dis' the Shitty.

The Shitty shapes you. Also many greats come from the Shitty.

In fact, all the greats come from the Shitty...

The first freedom fighter I knew was Paul Robeson, whose ballad 'Deep River' anchored me so strongly. Each texture, each note of the ballad was as if the river was within me as I swayed to the deep moving currents...

There were many others, each fighting for a better day.

~

Battles were also played out in the economics strata – no jobs = loitering = harassment = prison.

It seemed to be about race issues, and it was having a profound effect on mental health.

I spoke to my mother about this. I remember as a child asking my mother – even at that age I was aware...

"Mother, why is that man walking like that?"

"He got a bad leg, son."

The man was walking on his knees with a lunatic look on his face, smiling at everyone. I just knew he had lost something but I didn't know what as you saw many drunkards here on the estate. In fact, alcohol rules the roost all round...

Even whilst struggling to survive after I left the school and was still a child, I was aware of the racism towards black people from people of colour.

Black on black... the biggest silla...

There seemed to be a strata, and we were at the bottom for no apparent reason that I could figure out as I had not been told of my past yet.

Even the mental health hospitals up and down the country had a high number of KMT patients.

Likewise prisons.

One day a friend told me about a film called 'Roots' about slavery.

It was like a light switch.

In the ghetto the children were all super angry and ready to fight anyone, even themselves. This I did not partake in, but loved kin all the same.

This film does depict slavery that took place but if they did true research you would find indigenous black people living in the Americas and other far flung regions of the earth from the dawn of time...

...as we are a global race, not just from KMT.

Something was not quite right with it all.

There was contradiction in everything and it was causing me to keep moving, not realising it was everywhere.

This annoying, nagging thing was the fake history I was expected to swallow, a no-no of reality. Nothing made sense and I soon realised it was set up to keep most of the KMT people on the lower strata.

For example, if you really wanted to find out about ancient KMT you just communicated to the Ancestors.

Archaeologists just making the stuff up.

Some even saying we are not even from there.

Like the sculptures would lie...

As when you listen it's always 'maybe' or 'we think'.

I once saw a book in a charity shop called 'The Rape of the Pyramids'. I thought it a harsh title and did not get the book until two years later. I wish I had got it sooner as my thoughts are not alone...

RIVER CHANT

La Bissau di Guinea

La Cote

La Cote

La Bissau di Guinea

La Cote

La Cote

La Bissau di Guinea

La Cote

La Cote

La Bissau di Guinea

La Cote

La Cote

La Bissau di Guinea

La Cote

La Cote

La Bissau di Guinea

Ivoire

Ivoire

Noir ivoire...

[Flute & Shakers]

Back to school...

The routines were strange, and who cares about puffed out clouds, if you know what I mean.

The rain gains more attention.

It was always the same, as he grinds to a halt.

Paul, Paul, wait Paul – that last bit...

Grinds to a halt.

Do we need holy water?

I was too young to understand it all.

You could leave this place thinking you're gay.

He was a thin student, quite tall, athletic built.

He always came upon me. I didn't know what he was doing,

Till he suddenly stopped, slid off and went to his bed.

I never knew when he would come, but he always did...

And this student on top of me.

Like I said, I just laid there, still as I did not know what to do.

Confusion set in, which I have now recalled...

After leaving school, I had forgotten totally about it till writing the book.

It came as a jolt once this visual took form, a sensation of stillness – even though he was moving, I was always still, not even thinking, just still...

I hadn't ever discussed it till now, I think.

It's a bastard for sure, a seasoned conker to be had...

Paul, how do you feel about gays?

I don't think about gays.

Being a certain way is all part of the bigger picture.

The dogmatic intellectual will reason it away as an illness...

when secretly is *batti him a duck.*

Paul, that was brash...

I seen it on TV, a man calling them *evil battyman muss dead.*

Some get stoned ...

Would you like some counselling?

What for?

For what happened to you at school …

No, really, I'm okay...
Anyway, he didn't do anything else.
It was always the same...
I'm black an' macho so don't give me that gay bollocks.

Do I need counselling, shit...
I know what this is about.
You want me to say he rammed me.
No, never.
Sorry to disappoint you with a lack of sensationalism...

It's alright, Paul. Just breathe in... ho, and out.

EXTRACTS OF THE OTHER

Beyond the chains
Beyond the empires
Beyond the new names was a place.

Words fall short. Maybe in this place I will hum a lot, make sudden noises then go completely silent, swaying to an elemental ballad.

Then I'd dig some clay and make a sphere, cook it for so, so long till it melts.

Then I'd run around and say, look everyone I've found a meteorite.

Then I'd walk to the blue, green, orange, all-colour flower forest where milk and honey doth flow...

This land, this rock, rocky rockscapes.
Misty rock.
Going, going, gone.
The diamonds are ginger beer.
The gems shit nuggets.
Whilst you dig, dig, dig, dig, dig, dig, dig, the Ticka.
From dusk till dawn.

And I'm gonna tell Mami.

Mami comin'.

I called her an' told her.

I say, *"Mami, dem shit nugget hunters makin' too much noise, even the animals can't sleep."*

An' Mami says, "Watch this."

And a storm did stir and blew all the shit nugget hunters away forever...

Back to school...

When I was 15 I met a man who worked at the school, preparing students for leaving and sheltering in the outside world. He even did some training.

It's the first time I saw a physically disabled man in an important role.

Prior to seeing him, most disabled people in the '80s were mostly ignored.

So I really became aware of him.

He was so natural, it's hard to believe now.

Paul, what are the consequences for children growing up in these residential homes, if any?

I don't have a specific answer, just an awareness that has shaped certain manners, views, aspirations.
The teachers did their best,
I suppose...

~

Dear Nigga Paul, your accent's fake...
Middle English.

Ah, what's that?
Yu trine ta fit in ha?
They dun tole yu
yu speak like di queen
juss com outa cambridge
a black yuppee.

All because I like Milky Bars...

Dear Nigga Paul, it's not your choice.

Trine ah fit in.
What yu want with it?
Aint yu learn yet?
How long you been doin that sambo smile to fit in?
Ide imagine most of your life, eh?
It's not even a real sambo smile.
Yu not pullin the lips back enough,
like some o them butter head sambos.

Sometimes I wonder if they'll ever recover...

You're wrong.

I give a good sambo smile all the while.

They'll never catch me out.

That's what they want...

To see a sad sambo.

Well, they won't.

For the conditions are better, even with shampoo...

GHETTO PLANNA

Trine ta leeve di Shitty...

But to my surprise there was a man at the gate saying,

You cyan leeve di Shitty.

When yu baarn in di Shitty is deah yu staiy.

Was this gangster saying I couldn't leave the Shitty?

I had to think quick – then I had an idea.

I told him I'm taking Shitty with me on a vacation around the world.

He smiled and past we went, me and Shitty.

I thought it would be easy, but Shitty started to complain, *ha mek fuss.*

So mi tek Shitty back to di ghetto, an leeve Shitty...

Right there.

About six months later, I received a postcard from Shitty...

Yow fya king iya fya, wi de pon lockdown.

Yu afi cum back adi Shitty...

I promptly wrote back stating my new life had no place for Shitty.

I swiftly received another postcard calling me a sell-out and *marma* man, so I went straight back to the Shitty to make peace with Shitty.

The first thing I noticed, the Shitty was clean, neat, fresh, regal, up-market.

Yow Shitty waapen ah yu dis?

Yah mon wi eena di ites nung,

ital mek vital dance.

Shitty mi gaan.

Is love still...

Putting that aside...

I thrived on the creative side.

Being inspired by the 1st culture to share this wonder, I feel at one with the elements.

~

In 2015, quite recently, and in 1994 and 2004, I have had encounters with the law which should have been dealt with but weren't, even though I went to the CAB and spoke to a retired police sergeant who said the officers broke all the protocols and I had a strong case.

This situation has happened 5 times, and each time I have done nothing at all but to exist. This is what the elements tell me.

For example, I went into a store to buy something and I had a receipt for other goods.

The lady on the till saw me come into the store with the fruit and receipt – it's sometimes good to be local...

Well, as soon as I left the store, I walked for 2 minutes up the road and two police appeared from the shop. I had seen them go into the store as I was about to go in but was chatting to an old fisherman outside with the fruit in my hands, which they both looked at as they went into the store.

Well, they approached me and said I had stolen the fruit from the store. I was so in shock I didn't fully take it in. I said, "No – here is the receipt. It's Co-op fruit I have here not Lidl's."

Before I knew it, without resisting, I was arrested, handcuffed and dragged back to the store. I was in pain as the handcuffs were too tight. By the time we got to the store my whole arm was numb and tingling. I cried and cried for him to release them.

This is what he turned around and said...

"If you want fuckin' pain, I will give you..."

I was crying so loud because the pain was really bad. Eventually, a man came over and said, "You can't treat people like that." He was told to go away.

Another witness, who is an old man, pleaded with the officer, who spoke to the store manager, then the handcuffs were loosened and eventually taken off.

As I stood up, this strange energy came over me that told me this was against basic human rights and they were not here to help but to destroy what little peace is left on the Earth... Why?

~

I went home and cried and was told to go to the hospital as I was not good.

When I went to the hospital and explained that I had hurt my wrist and my arm felt numb and kept tingling, the nurse asked what I had done.

I told her I had been arrested and then freed... she went completely silent, treated me, then she let me go.

~

Now, this might sound odd, but for the next couple of months that arm was not good...

I could not do my work properly.

It would tingle and ache for hours, coming and going.

Some people knew about it and demanded that I seek justice.

I did not have the confidence, but a time came when I did feel the urge to seek justice. I followed the advice of the retired police sergeant at the CAB.

It was quite odd that it was a retired police sergeant who told me that the officers had broken every single protocol.

All leads I took I was humiliated...

The solicitor who he told me to seek advice from told me...

"You can't afford to sue the police!" and put the phone down.

The thing was, I never mentioned suing the police, but I felt this is where it would go eventually but, as I've stated, I'm an elemental man and on previous encounters where they have been totally rough and over-the-top, I have said through a mediator worker, I just want to be left alone.

Now listen to this... I actually believed that they would put a picture on the wall and say, 'Leave this man alone – he does not want any trouble. He's not into fashion, just a basic guy.'

Nope...

Again...

I was dragged off the streets, only this time I was coming from the local college where I taught music to special needs students two days a week.

On the way home, waiting for a lift, 2 police officers jumped out of their car and one of them grabbed my arm.

I panicked and started to run. Before I knew it, I had lots of plain-clothes officers on my case. They pinned me down as I collapsed in panic. They asked why did I run.

I said, "You are always targeting me and each time I've done absolutely nothing wrong."

The shock...

In my bag were two large wooden masks from the college that I had made. These were heavy masks with indented shells and other materials.

Both masks were smashed and the shells were all gone. You could see where they had been hit on the pavement.

I have had a few more encounters but I get depressed writing them down as all I wanted was to be left alone...

Again, I was told I looked like a drug dealer from Bristol... a black drugs dealer.

But what I did find hard to believe is all the files on the Lidl case from the hospital are gone – lost or destroyed – just like my art work.

I was now being told plainly there is no justice for me to get peace for any of these transgressions.

If I transgress to anyone I feel very bad and will try to make peace by good intentions where possible.

That incident made me quit working at schools and going out. I became completely paranoid. Even the people who I lived with were worried and sought help for me.

So all these incidents were meant to crush me for some apparent reason, because this is what it does... breaks you down.

Po dinq

Laugh, now laugh

Laugh at the black suspect

Don't you know me, suspect black?

I'm always stopped and being punished for being you.

The black drugs dealer from Bristol is the favourite one.

The black suspect drinks milk and reads the newspapers.

He also shits, cleans his teeth and, believe it or not, can swim.

The black suspect is on the move. Where's he going? To commit a crime? Let's see...

Hey look, he's crossed the road, has suspect black.

Suspect black approaches a tree. Maybe he has a stash in there.

Suspect black is looking at the tree in full bloom and smiles.

Now he's getting into a car. Is that his car, and are those his kids and puppy?

The children and puppy are playing in the back seat.

Ho look, black suspect is stroking his chin and sighing. Thinking of a robbery, maybe?

But the children and puppy?

They'll just have to come along.

Black suspect drives down a few more streets then stops the car near a school.

Oh no, black suspect is going to rob the school.

Something strange is happening here, and I need to pause to take it in.

4 more black suspects show up with kids.

Oh no, they're all getting out of their cars.

It's bigger than we thought, the nursery as well...

It's time to leave.

THE DESCRIPTION ...

- Short, stout, woolly hair, big lips – Black.
- Tall, thin-faced with beard – Black.
- Athletic build, medium height square chin – Black.
- Lawyer, wears a suit, has a neat beard – Black.
- Doctor, wears a suit, no beard – Black.
- Broad-faced, chubby, dark-skinned – Black.
- Young-faced young adult, mixed race – Black.
- Middle-aged designer – Black.
- Old-aged pensioner, over 60 – Black ...

CUYA ['look at this']

Where are we?

Hey you, from Ancestor.

Who are you?

Cannot you see mon – monji mon, the Ancestors are vexed.

They stir the dry soil, barren the fertile land, set the demons loose, kick the lazy lion and sing a bitter sound none can abide.

Ba konga chikungo chikungo the broken pot laughs, laughs into the future whilst you struggle with the past.

Gloomy bush weed dances a crude twist whilst the yellow sun sparkles platinum.

ASAP – nope.

Are you black, sir?

Purple black.
Blue black.

What is black, sir?

Negro black.
Sambo black.
Tobacco black.
Rum black.

You're black, are you?
Do you have that tight magnetic hair?
Do you recall pillage – displacement?

Dear blackie, I used to love you but you turned out a bastard like the rest, saying, "Kin, kin, look how they treat us," then you betray the cause.

You're not coming to my party no more.

Never.

You're not playing with my toys, they're mine.

Also, you guessed it,

I'm telling Mami.

I'll say, *"Mami – you see that good fi nutten spyaga bwoi? Is dem ah whole we back, dont?"*

And mami will say, "Watch this."

And spyaga ah nyam rockstone fi yood [food]...

~

I was informed that I was not acting black enough.

You mean like speaking Black?

Acting Black?

What kind of Black would you prefer me to be?

Do you have a preference?

We already were upper-middle-class status, and I can speak like them, so let me be with it.

You're jealous, jealous, I can be understood and you can't.

I've seen you pretending to fit in as soon as another spade appears. You're out of there mentally and physically – no association necessary.

This is why I say what Blackie would you prefer me to be?

What kind of Black?

You mean like you?

No thank you!

I've seen this pattern before.

Although retro pink won't let me in, I'll pretend to be accepted and play along with everyone else!

Man, that's sad, and you said you'd never be a sad sambo.

Well, if pretending to be accepted isn't a sad sambo then what is?

Bro', you right, it's a sad situation, but still I won't show them a sad sambo – never – although they see a sad sambo every minute and wish it away!

Is he still here! I thought you'd moved.

Yes, I get the point!

But are we not friends?

Yes, we are.

So why wish me away?

Because you're poor, and I hate the poor!

Did you really just say that?

Yes...

Yeah, their burden is blocking the flood.

Who said they could leave the Shitty?

I cried a sambo river for you, so please let me in.

I like the soaps and mirrors (not the pet bit), or baths and showers – ha, here comes Uncle Tickle with retro pink!

Uncle Pickle, how long have you been with retro pink?

40 years.

Do you see anything else?

Nope!

What about a Creole Amazonian?

Nope, it has to be retro pink.

Cho!

I'm telling Mami.

Mamii.

Mamii.

Mamii.

I callin'.

Mami come.

"Mami, is Uncle Tickle well?"

"No, son, he's not well. He has an illness called punanilitus of the retro pink disorder. Tis a serious ting as he believe only retro pink can satisfy him to the fullest. I been tellin' Uncle Tickle all these years, leave retro pink alone, even when 'im get ban im go back fi di retro pink, seh hey Uncle Tickle you nuh like we agen?"

Uncle Tickle seh, retro pink rule. Retro Pink, you've zombied Uncle Tickle. What do you really want from him?

I have it already!

Is weh you have already?

Im sugar stick – Mami was right.

~

Just the other day, a friend told me about applying for funds for Black Artists. 'Go on, King Kong, it's your rights.'

The way she said King Kong!

She's off my list and, guess what?

I'm telling' Mami – Retro Pink's in trouble for the first time ever.

Mami's comin'.

I called her an' told her.

I said, "Mami, you see that Retro Pink there called me King Kong."

Mami became a bird and landed on Retro Pink's shoulder, who wailed and passed out.

Retro Pink had a dream. She was being chased by thousands of naked black men with wide open eyes. It looked like they ate Retro Pink for sport. Just as one landed upon her, Retro Pink was gone. She woke up and became a skin tone collaborator.

But getting back to King Kong – what is this? Do I resemble King Kong, or in her mind am I linked in some way to King Kong? Let's go and find out...

Paul, there is an association with your people and King Kong. It goes way, way back. Even when I was a child black people were referred to as monkeys.

Thank you!

Now I can eat bananas with confidence...

Back to school...

During my final years of school and regularly going home for some if not most weekends, I began to see a pattern of the estate and school as two separate places. One was kind of a recluse, the other the Shitty. When leaving the Shitty and going back to school, I always felt in a strange way as if the Shitty did not want me to go back, but I had to go back as it was my home.

I discussed this with Mother one time, about the backwards and forwards, as either place was not where I now lived.

The school was kind to me a lot, but in other ways I hated it. At home it was the same. I had a strong resentment of being where you are not really wanted.

Mother was gentle, firm, calm as always, and told me that I will not be at school or living at home forever and that one day I will move and have my own place.

Could I live in my place? Was I prepared in any way? The school had prepared me, us, for the outside world, but it would be a struggle to adapt fully.

On the opening days of the school, always in summer, I remember vividly you would get to see your friends' parents, showing them your dwellings, then it would be all over before it started. It would also leave a funny sensation when they left as you too wanted to go home.

I had mixed feelings when at school, but I settled down with routine, activities, and my own space, which as an adult has a similar frequency! I enjoy the space to work and observe the wonders that always seem to have me in awe.

SPAID RELIEF

If you have ever been called a Coconut by a fellow Planet of the Apes then this relief fund is for us – I mean you...

Did it leave you feeling like...

Why the fuck do I bother with these chicken-loving shrimps?

Take the relief and build your confidence again.

Putting this aside...

As I said, I thrived on the creative side.

Being inspired by an ancient civilisation of the cosmos and earth, I felt at one with elements...

But the fossil tree knows the path of the old bone.

I observed society, how it functions on a basic level and the economic strata.

Race strata – my mind was opening up to how society works and my place in it...

It was small, small learning, but I was beginning to recognise certain references to people of colour and my place in all of this...

My cosmic grandma used to say, "Know your place," which I instinctively understood, but I still did not fit in too much as I realised that life was going to be hard with all this baggage.

History.

The knowing your place would reveal itself later...

Looking back now, yes, it was a harsh introduction, but on another level, the elemental level, I found no borders, just the natural beauty of life and its wonders.

And I stuck by this close connection with nature because nature is the teacher on all levels of the body and cosmos.

This is evident in the achievements I gained from this school and some of the experiences I have shared with you.

PERRY AID

You. Yes, you!

Now listen.

Now you see.

Now you hear.

Now you smell, smell it all cooking.

Did you smell it before?

Pass time with it?

It can't talk and won't.

See that hill over there?

That's its ass...

Blackie knows about selling charcoal from the moon.

Hey you!

Where did you get that honesty from?

It's banned.

The frequency battle was on the news tonigh'.

What! Stop... stop...

INTERVIEW... 1991 BRITTANY

The artist is working on a sculpture project in Brittany, at the foundry of Jacques 'Menu', forging the metals for working the granite.

Jacques 'Menu' is a short man with a fiery temperament.

It was at this foundry where the interview took place...

Paul, what brings you to Brittany?

Well, firstly I like the breads they have here. Also, the Bretons seem more tolerant than the French.

Aren't they the same people?

Can we talk about the project please?

Paul, is it true you stole snow from the sky?

No, it was mistaken identity – works every time. I have never stolen snow from anyone or from anywhere.

What is the duration of this project?

I would say around 4 years; it's non-technical. Once we have all materials it should all run smoothly.

Do you speak French?

Well, yes... yes, I do.

What can you say in French, Paul?

Paul.

Anything else?

Le ciel... bonjour... comment est vous...

Yes, that's French.

To be honest, interviewer, I'm not really feeling what you're saying... Or is it me? Some questions sound empty.

I'm sorry, Paul, I was told to go slow because of the autism you're on -

Who told you that?

You did.

Ho...

Well, it is so... not an imbecile – genuine autism spectrum. I did want to know, but now I'm not concerned much with it all.

And, guess what?

I'm tellin' Mami.

Although Mami knows...

I'm still tellin' Mami.

I'll say, *"Mami, them good fi nutten social recka nah mek e wuk..."*

An Mami says, "Shut up."

I go quiet for a while.

Then I'll say, *"Mami...*

...is who ya tek fi fooool?"

"Ah pikni run tings. Is dat a gwaan yu seet?"

"Yaa mi mada, is love still. Cah ah yu gidi I foundation still."

Di next ting mi know smaddi liff i arf di groun ahn dash I eena sorrel bush.

When mi com out all scratch an ting, mi look up an see one raas rino.

Mi juss run up di nearest tree an rhino ah wait dung below.

Well, I never...

So mi have a plan.

Mi shout dung rhino, rhino.

Hear weh rhino say...

Don't shout, man – mi eers too sensitive!

Fram up here I can see plenty wasp...

Rhino gaan...

EXTRACT FROM MAUVE SCRIPT

Yes, there are communities, but these names...

yellow communities - mauve communities - retro communities - blackie communities, and - cerulean communities

...all living side by side in perfection.

Mauve took care of that.

Let's explore mauve's community...

Yow, mauve is weh yu ah se?

Mauve, yes blaka we not spose fi mix...

Mauve uptown, mi bredda.

We cleen eena retro.

But you blackie juss waan com een.

Yu tink retro really, really like unnu?

Retro fed up wid yu raas an waan sen yu bak ah bush.

Bout yu ah British.

Which part dat?

Mussi di cacafaat presentation society sen e...

Mauve, listen.

You don't need to give me the Shitty slang.

I knows yuse educated.

But heer dis...

Yu know di spectrum sweet

an di mystry set

dat fram di darkness comes di light...

It's not that, blackie.

Mi know yu element.

Retro tell everyone secret bout you, only yu don't know it...

For generations yu don't know it.

So some ah walk bout like duppy ah grab any kinda ism an scism fi satisfy dem dry up raas.

132

An yu see di mauve range, retro range, lilac range, lime green range, an di yellow range, dem seh blackie range too dark...

I said to the little blackie princess, it's not true, it's not true.

Mauve's a spastic and still sleeps with Mami going on 18.

Who wants to be a mauve spastic?

Mauve, yu so spiteful, pretending like yu something; yu just a mauve.

See how you stir things, mauve.

You're so false.

I heard ochre been addressing this morning 'no sir', 'im of the lighter ochre range, a cousin of mauve...

Mi juss buss out an laugh.

Look ow mauve tun ocra eena eedyat.

Juss look how mauve ah fool everybody.

So important mauve...

A cousin of royal purple.

You know what, mauve?

You're all the same... private crime.

You're all thieves.

Lime green and lilac, they're very bad.

Look at them, and you with your burgundy associates.

Anti-mauve – nope.

~

The Shitty now stands tall, starched and hungry.

Welfare wont feed it.

Nor the bishop!

O Shitty, it's past tribal.

Past gangs.

Past the new faces.

Your neighbourhood shines its own light.

Along with the rats...

Can't you see, Shitty, we will always be a part of society, mainstream or not.

It's how we live in the Shitty.

So close in proximity some bad frequency ha' mix'.

An di place map out...

Wid di sweet little hustle fi tek ah nex high.

Cyaan com down.

Cyaan com down.

Di baastad drone ah fall fram di sky.

An di car boot ah sell passport.

Water – water used to be water...

Used to be a step in the right direction.

With a focus and purpose.

The ants have it, the bees have it, the birds have it.

But your purpose...

Your living empire purpose...

Oh, Mami.

Mamiiiiii!

Mami did not reply.

It is quiet.

So still.

The only sound now is frequency.

Now I hear Mami.

First it is a gentle trickle sound recalling brooks.

Sounding now like gentle crystal bells swinging to Ella.

Then a sweet mento sound recalling rural olde Jamaica where lilac, mauve and cerulean still lord it...

This mento music, long before reggae and ska, has elements of both in it, and yet it is still a distinct form of musical rhythms.

As I listen to the variants in mento, a priest appears...

Carrying a shaker and a stick.

The stick is pure yellow, metal – gold.

And the shaker luminates as if conversing with the priest.

It is only when I look into the priest's face that I realise it is that man that was in the psychiatric ward, high on medication, dribbling on his top and mumbling strange words.

The Ancestors helped him, there's no other way to that transformation.

Now he's looking at me, staring.

I feel the frequency of him; we have synced, and communicate as one, no words necessary.

We are in an open space. The land is flat. You can see for miles.

As I am taking in this landscape there is a sensation and we are gone.

What I am getting from the priest is that place where we stood is a place of departure and arrival.

What's interesting about this face, the priest's face, is that I see also in his face...

MAMI

OSCAR PETERSON

JOAN ARMATRADING

MILES DAVIS

QUEEN CANDACE

TREVOR MCDONALD

JOSEPHINE BAKER

KING TUBBY

ROKIA TROARE

FRANTZ FANON

DIANA ROSS

LAUREN HILL

SHIRLEY BASSEY

TELLIMA CUOCERE

RICHARD PRIOR

NANA MAROON

PAUL BOGLE

CARL LEWIS

TAMSIN ARCHER

BERNIE GRANT

CRAIG CHARLES

WHOOPI GOLDBERG

JOSE BALIMO

JAMES BROWN

WALTER RODNEY

MAMA B

LEWIS HAMILTON

ROLAND KIRK

JIMMY CLIFF

LADY DAY

...the list goes on and on.

All these faces seem to be one face.

Here they seem all to be as one but back on earth are seriously divided.

Who or what is blocking the frequency, if it is being blocked at all?

ANTI MAUVE?

Nope.

It's just, for some unknown reason, mauve wants to let everyone know he's mauve.

Mauve, the twat.

Hey blackie... I heard that from 4 pages away!

Why yu so vex, blackie, ee?

Is weh lex yu?

No, mauve. Why you speakin like us?

You really wanna know, mauve?

Yes, if it helps the situation.

Burgundy wants to take me to court. I've no chance.

Burgundy literally owns all the judges.

I shouldn't have listened to that yellow inspector.

You knew all along...

Oh look, cerulean and blackie are friends and are going for a walk together.

The cerulean community are eco-friendly and know blackie's mysteries.

This transitional studio.

Purple questions got it.

Some say amethyst.

Either, either.

Yellow is blue...

The money was silent, but when it spoke, *studio vex an lex*.

Nuh worry yu self.

Manana yu bruk agen...

This pikni ya always ah chat.

GOING MAINSTREAM

For the past 30 years, I have been working in schools and colleges off and on from nursery to adult education.

When I first came into teaching it was through my artworks, all of which were natural.

I did not have to go to meetings, although I was given a part-time contract to work at a college, which I did for a few years.

This was invaluable as I communicated through my work, the work of teacher, whether in music or sculpture.

I was given opportunities to work and share what I had learned, and I really liked it.

Although I was teaching, they were collaborative activities, be they music, sculpture or gardening.

And whilst working in schools and colleges, they valued my approach to materials and students.

Most of the students were special needs children and adults with special needs.

I found the special needs approach to materials like clay was direct and honest. There were thought processes and what I found with the ceramic sculptures was the bases were absent, meaning the pieces were meant to find their own balance, or the piece was the balance itself...

When I was making ceramic sculptures in the early days, I did not consider bases and was told to consider them if I wanted the pieces to stand...

I took the advice and make my own style of bases.

Whilst teaching in these institutions of education, I thought, in a special needs school where qualifications don't exist, you just have to be.

So when I found myself side by side with qualified teachers, I found I could communicate through my work, and I have been fortunate to have met good people that have helped on all levels.

It makes me wonder where are my friends from the school now...

Did they too have the imbecile badge?

Aside from this...

In 2002, someone called me a Sculptor, and I didn't fully know what it meant.

I had to go look it up. I only knew about the large, public statues.

In 1987, I had this urge to create experimental art.

That same year, I beheld the clay, and that was the start of the atavist elemental...

I remember being given some chisels and a mallet.

I plunged straight into the wood, which I promptly burnished with fire and put the pieces away.

Once I had a body of work in these pieces, I was asked to be part of an art exhibition in a big old school which was no longer used.

I chose a room to put my work in.

A complete shrine emerged, which had press coverage.

Two gentlemen from the British Museum came to the opening, along with the Mayor.

The two gentlemen asked me where I got my style inspiration from for these pieces.

I mentioned something about the past and feeling my way.

They told me that the pieces were almost identical to some they had, and asked had I copied them?

When I told them I'd never seen the pieces before, they understood...

It was my father from which these pieces emerge...

The ancient KMT.

Because I did not grow up with him he came to me often in dreams.

The interesting thing is that these dreams were clan-like. It was always men, sitting, some standing, doing ceremonies.

I remember being at a few of them and not even questioning their presence, but I always awoke with a KMT presence, without a doubt.

This is where I got to be with my father on another level, of another time and place.

Even in my artworks, I had this innate feeling to burnish the wood, sometimes beating crushed stones into them or a pigment paste, creating encrustations.

What came back looking at me said one thing...

Go leegro – when I started with stone, wood and metal, but when I worked the clay and all its possibilities, the clay was the final cog.

I have seen some fine sculptors doing the rounds.

I remember one time exhibiting at a show in London and I met a Kenyan sculptor who had some small samples of soapstone art.

Very elemental.

His work, although abstract, had a distinct primal order and mysticism.

When we were talking, he promptly sold them to a man visiting the gallery.

When seeing creative people doing artworks, I always look for a central sound in frequencies.

All of my elemental works, pieces, have a distinct atavist presence, which began with father's genetic, cosmic input as I had met my father at 14.

I remember my brother telling me one weekend we were going to see Dad, but not to tell Mum.

Dad. What did that mean?

All those nights in the coal bunker, the beatings...

Lack of food.

Fear.

What is father?

Is it a place?

I was 14 and we boarded the bus and travelled for a long time, then we walked for a while to an estate.

My brother rang a bell and the door opened.

What I saw I will never forget.

As I stood looking straight, all I saw was legs.

By the time I got to his face I was looking up quite high.

Father was around 7 feet in height, and I froze, as I had never seen a giant before.

I remember him putting one of his large arms around my shoulder and gently welcoming us inside.

I was still in awe and physical wonder, and curiosity.

This is when the first anatomy lesson began.

My brother and I sat on the sofa and my father went to get refreshments.

When he walked away, I didn't speak. I was silent.

Then he came back into the room and put the tray on the table.

When he went to sit down, it was almost mechanical because of his height.

I really took him in but didn't say much...

It was all happening on another level.

I do remember how warm he was, with a deep rumbling voice and a very ancient, large, oval face with a huge nose. It's quite odd – I have my mother's features but my father's essence...

Well, after my brother and I talked with father, it was time to leave, promising to return another day.

When he stood up to go to the door, this time I was really watching him. He had a distinct, ancient presence around him, and had around 30 children, and me and my brother were two of them, as my uncle informed me one day...

Yu father we call him giraffe when him was likkle bwoy cah he was tall even den...

When we left, I was in another space as the new word Father was born.

I had to nurture this term now that I had met him. It would be three years till I saw him again.

But within these three years I had many dreams about him and his ancient race...

I didn't know then I would be doing elemental works.

But I felt KMT was the centre of it.

As I grew into a man, the first thing I noticed was his presence got stronger, the cosmic essence more clarified. The elemental work seemed to know where we were going. The themes were always present of the KMT, as it was, and is, a global issue...

My work in this sphere is to tell of a past the best I can and this is through the art...

It's just an awareness of another way of seeing my past.

And even this epic task is no easy task. A history as cemented in the past, in the institutions from the past, and people study this past and impose it upon you, when in reality it doesn't fit.

You can go online and see how many sites have debates about how our history was stolen and a new one given, denying our cosmic past.

This is not possible, as we are finding out today...

CHILDHOOD WONDERS

It was one of those moments in childhood where something happens that you, and only you, will enjoy to the fullest.

Mine was when I was 7. I was standing on a bank.

It was sunny, nice and bright, and a butterfly landed on my shoulder and said the word 'artist'...

It was strange, because after that I had an infinity with butterflies and expected them to land on me, which they still do sometimes.

So going back to my teens, no, I didn't know or think about art.

Even when I started out working, I still didn't see it as art.

This realisation came much, much later, maturing like a wine, it took its own time.

The visuals of these ancient places where the artefacts had origins seemed so ancient it could have been another dimension, and whenever I touched the materials the journey would begin.

It's like I went there for confirmation of pieces in situ to be used.

For example, in 2014 I sent a proposal for a contemporary ceramic expo.

I had already journeyed and saw the artefacts, but it wasn't the artefacts that I fully embraced, it was this ancient ritual that I observed whist being there.

The scene was in an arid location, hot and high up.

My viewing was on a bank looking down on the ritual.

There is a small building symmetrical in shape in an open space. The building has an opening, no door.

A group of ancient men formed a wide circle.

They are still and it is hot.

From the building emerges an ancient old woman, following her a girl.

When the girl enters the circle the wind changes.

She's generating something...

The artefacts are brought out from the building, all 9 of them, and are placed within a circle of their own.

The artefacts, about half a metre in height and 20 inches in width, they all have legs as bases and seem like ceramic or stone. They are not figurative, they don't represent anything you would see today. Even the colouring seemed new.

Back to the girl...

It seems the old woman is her assistant as this child seems to work the elements.

As the child walks around the circle the wind picks up. The ancient men walk anti clockwise in the opposite direction to the child.

Then I see it...

The artefacts are generating a frequency and are now off the ground vibrating a sound. As the sound gets deeper I

145

notice the child simply vanishes and the artefacts become silent and still...

The journey visuals have passed, and I now produce my interpretation...

Once I began to interpret the visuals to produce a body of work, things were revealed that I hadn't seen, for example the ancient men wore what looked like metal hats close to the scalp. Their features were of another time and place. Likewise both the woman and girl had an atavist presence, and the rituals seemed standard practice.

This creative practice that had endless energy, ancient, I felt it from the start but couldn't name it.

The realisation that it was called art seemed at odds with the practice.

The term Artist is standard...

CERAMICA, THE FELDSPAR CYCLE

I have consistently worked making materials from earth minerals, extracting minerals – Calcites, pigments like Haematite, Limonite, Manganese ores from the old tin and silver mines, aquatic minerals that are full of Manganese dioxide – iron ores – oxides from a variety of stones, soils, clays, and various sands, from course to extra fine, also in a vast range of colours. I have a large collection of feldspar crystals, processed minerals and pigments, all for the clay bodies.

These materials that I use are found in the shallow granite riverbeds, coastal paths, woods, beaches, hedgerows, paths, gardens, excavation sites, valleys, quarries – these are the places where I source most of my materials, and I carry everything as I don't drive. This I have done for 30 years and it has kept me very well, 'working' out clay bodies, mineral compositions, and of course firing chambers, Raku – brick kilns, chimneys, 'Barrel' pits, and sawdust.

I sampled a range of paper kilns, which is a great project for children as you paint the clay onto the wood and paper armature.

I fired one and the rain came down heavy so I had to stand over it till the rain stopped. Luckily it did, and the firing was complete.

I am making outdoor firing chambers to fire my own processed clay which I make shock proof as I tend to pull them out like in Raku.

I gave a demonstration in 2018 for Raku outdoor firing.

After about an hour into the firing, I promptly pulled it out of the fire and plunged it into water. The hissing and spitting sound made you think it would shatter, but not this clay.

I studied the patina, then put it back in the fire.

People came up asking, why didn't it break?

I told them it's thermal shock-proofing...

Some of them asked for the recipe.

The work as an ancient presence...

With a strong, learned, natural and intuitive approach, this intuitive tool has helped me to understand building kilns and firing chambers. Outdoor kilns are as varied as numbers.

Some are basic, others complex.

I enjoy the fullness of ceramics, the many ways to fire a piece, making a body of work.

It is this language, sourcing the fuel from the old hedgerows and seasonal falling, old fallen oak and hazel trees. The fuel is ample, which I source, stack and clean for firing.

All this is a language of the elemental way.

It is a simple, natural way. A lot of work is involved in this collaboration.

Materials are provided. For example...

On my way to work one day, I came across a granite-sand waterfall. I was on my way to dig some up, and there it was – the bright yellow to cream white decomposed granite feldspar, both refined falling out from the high hedgerow, pushed by a badger ready for use...

This is how most of the materials present themselves for use...

One day I found a completely dried out oak tree felled years before. This seasoned oak wood kept me in fuel for some time.

Back to the elemental ways...

These ceramic artefacts are only fired one time to a high temperature of 1200. The heat climbs quite quickly, using a combination of heating fuels – wood – coal - organic matter, e.g. straw, sawdust, some in combination.

I have seen this firing in indigenous people's practice of firing i.e. South Korea - Japan – India - Abulan - Iran...

Notes on collaborative approach... Essence...

From the start of working out the creatives there has always been a presence in the elements.

These elements frequencies, which seem to be active in the process of sourcing materials and making these artefacts...

These kinds of collaborations are open to interpretation and are not of one concept.

Other input has added to the outcome of these artefacts.

Because the intuitive teacher can be found in most elements, both of land and aquatic, it is this vast learning space where the source is found.

The collaborative elements are the same frequencies that inform narratives.

The interpretation of the bodies of work are formed in this manner alongside journeys to some of the places of origin...

This is why I'm cross with Papua New Guinea.

And if I haven't told Mami already, I'm telling her right now...

Mami.

Mami.

I callin'.

Mami.

Mami comin'.

"Mami, why dem papuans turned crocodiles into guns?"

"They freedom fighters, son."

"What they fighting for, Mami?"

"Freedom, di crocodile tun gun..."

It was on one of these early journeys I got acquainted with the Papuan culture.

~

I have worked in Cararra marble since 1995.

It was a winter morning. As I went to the workshop, I could see leaning against the door a long block of white marble, which I later found out was Cararra marble.

After this, it seemed to be coming most of the time, and is one of my favourite stones for sculpture.

I was lucky enough to get to know the Youings, stonemasons of Barnstaple.

I used to go and watch the old men carve the stones, cut the stones and lettering of the stones.

It was all inspiring. Every single experience with these skilled masons was invaluable.

I did not visit the mason place for a few years but when I went again, the old man had passed away and his daughter from London had come down to clear out the building.

What she required from me was help to clear out the stones and tools, as it was a listed building – no change could be added or taken from it.

Well, this was a big task. I only said yes because she said her father had mentioned me and I was allowed some tools and stone.

But first I had to help and try to sell the surplus stone.

I knew of two good people from whom I sometimes buy one-off blocks of stone for sculpture. One was near Winkleigh. He really helped, and she liked him. Another friend, Renus from Broomhill Sculpture Park, also took some of her stock whilst I was helping him with restoration work.

Once the stock was nearly all gone, I was offered very old tools and some fine Cararra marble, from which I have carved some fine pieces and still do.

Prior to this, most of the stone work was granite and sandstone.

All with the strong atavist presence.

The work requires space, peace, patience for the collaboration to manifest.

No matter how far-stretched the themes and concept, the ancient presence is in it.

OPPORTUNITIES

I re-wrote this chapter a few times as the opportunities are boundless.

When I came into the arts I was like a bushman, very secretive for unknown reasons, but just producing the work.

On my first contact with outsiders, they were telling me I needed to exhibit. This didn't mean much.

Once I was informed I could have an exhibition and show the work, I went at it bushman style.

The installation was received well.

This was my first official showing of works.

The themes were ancient shrines and artefacts, inspired by some potent spirits of the elemental frequency which informed the works' direction and themes.

Until this time, it was always carved, encrusted wood in mixed medium, but at this time I was discovering the wonders of clay... which I have worked with ever since.

~

As I began to work my way through society with my works, I found that even in the arts an issue kept coming up.

This kind of stuff...

I was asked by museum staff to submit for a show there which would be very interesting geological art for both young and old. I submitted my proposal, and I was informed by the curator...

"We have our Sonia Boyce."

Now, all respect to Sonia Boyce, but this statement shows clearly how your progress can be hindered.

How can a curator of a museum make such a blatant statement – *tell me, nuh?*

...and guess what?

Yes, you guessed it...

I'm telling Mami, and Sonia Boyce.

I'll say, *"Mami, why is blackie taking all the cake?"*

And Mami says, "It's not your cake – and leave Sonia alone..."

And for the first time it felt like Mami was not on my side.

So 30 years later I went to Mami an' said...

"You right, Mami. It's not my cake."

But Mami says, "It's your cake too."

...and guess what?

I'm telling on Mami.

I'm not tellin' Dadi – he's a lunatic an' blows at the slightest wiff... No...

I'm telling Uncle Tickle.

Uncle Tickle was jet coal black but preferred retro pink, and yes, you guessed it, got banned...

I remember reading the email a few times and it honestly felt like an infant child had written it.

Most of the places that I thought would be a good place to show my work have been blocked.

Or I have been fobbed off.

I have had my own exhibitions and also in galleries, even joining art galleries for a while.

Penrith Gallery in St Ives was one where we had three shows per year.

But even this was all clichéd and weird, so I left it.

This was a good experience and I met some good artists, but something was not right with the art world, and this was bugging me.

It didn't seem real.

All clichéd, grouped off.

Favourites, like sports.

I was beginning to see my profession's cesspit called the art world...

Truth is, someone pressed the nigger button and all hell broke loose – without omelettes...

I was also informed by a gallery owner in London...

"You are on the wrong side."

These statements didn't bother me. They gave me an awareness of how people speak to you, because I have worked consistently for the past 30 years, often in difficult circumstances, and have learnt to just work and respect nature.

But the so-called blockage intrigued me and was also an issue for me as I wanted to move forward but couldn't yet see why I it was not happening.

Then it clicked one day...

and I have never looked back.

~

Away from this, I have been awarded on numerous occasions by the Arts Council funds to do more research on my ceramic study approach to materials, as I make and explore mineral properties.

I spend a lot of time at the rivers, shallow rivers.

Although working, I am aware of the rhythm and sound of the water and am always stilled by its frequency.

Also, I feel the child in me is still alive, as something inside that stopped, or never started, as I see and experience life in abstract, not black and white.

I still have not had that man feeling.

It's just an existence of sound manifestations, all within their own cycles, aside man-made time.

Why is man so obsessed with man-made time?

I see and feel detached from humanity.

Although I have feelings, the overall expression is to get away from it all, not in a planned or thought-about way, but a natural way, and try to be this way as close as possible.

It's a new dawn.

An old song.

As stated previously on many pages, I am close to the elements and most of my life is this way.

This realisation followed me into adulthood, that I'm not going to change and this is the way I am.

That man thing that's supposed to happen to you – the voice changing, the acne, the putting away of childhood, whatever – none of these came as I watched all my peers develop past me.

Did this have something to do with the food I ate at the school?

Or that the tests I had as a child confirmed this?

I have many questions, but do not seek an answer.

The work is different though – it wants out.

People comment on the work and I try to be my best round them, being polite and talking about the things they see, even working alongside other artists.

There are a few books and lots of brochures on previous shows that I have exhibited or set up on my own. This I enjoy.

In 2019 I set up a show which was a complete success all round, and I am still reeling from it.

The prep involved in me setting up this show goes as follows...

LOCATION...

I had seen this building on the harbour and kept passing it. I always have an eye for buildings as workspaces.

Well, one day I asked the harbour master if it would be possible to do an exhibition in there.

To my surprise, the harbour master said yes.

So we had a talk and the dates were set.

Because it was a harbour and most, if not all, of my work is elemental landscape and seascape based, the title was 'Land of Sea' with the themes: land - aquatic - fossil – mammal - pigments.

Materials were: ceramic - white marble – elemental pigment paints - white bone...

I went away and in 4 months I had produced a body of work. Now, this body of work is a mystery to most people, as out of every single person I asked, "How long do you think it would take to produce this body of work?" most said 3 years.

Even our son said this.

It was only when I told them how I work then they kind of understood what I meant.

Something happens when you're in a works creative.

In the early days, I tried to visualise its presence, as it is a collaboration, and the more I put in the less difficult it became.

For example, all the marble sculptures were hand-worked, no machines involved.

Looking at these blocks of marble is 3 years' work, not forgetting the making and firing of ceramics and, of course, the pigment paintings.

All this work is not physically possible.

What happens?

What is the process for this?

One night, around 4.00 am in the studio, I was rasping a marble piece and I looked at my hand and the speed it was rasping it could have been a machine.

Yes, I felt it but was more intrigued by it, as this is the process in this space when you're given a date to create a body of work.

Things just come together – the marble, the clay, the pigments and fire all produced this body of work.

Now this was it. The work was complete. I had a van driver as the work was produced on the moors and was going to a harbour town 70 miles away.

Well, that Saturday the driver never showed up.

I still had 5 days to set up.

I rang him and he mentioned a late night and that tomorrow, Sunday, was good.

That Saturday night, sitting with the packed works ready to go, was necessary as I hadn't stopped the whole time and I felt a good creative frequency around the work as I was honouring the elements.

Well, when we loaded up, he decided to take the scenic route and kept stopping and taking it all in.

I thought to myself, what a way to bring the work. He is such a funny, mellow, hard-working Slovac man.

Well, we got to the coastal town down to the harbour. There were Morris dancers everywhere.

I remember looking at his expression. We unloaded, had a drink, and he drove back to the moors whist I planned the layout, etcetera.

I needed a large tiara plinth in the middle but I only had about 6 cubic ones, so I went to a friend in the town and he helped me to make a big one.

The way that theatre worker worked with his skill, I was happy and impressed.

Once complete, he just put it on top of his car, tied it down with guy ropes, and off we went.

I had already sorted out postcards of various sizes and other miscellaneous items – all the time in the back of my mind are thoughts of 'what next' to keep going on.

Another friend helped re-arrange my statement, whilst another friend corrected my listings of work and prices – the latter was corrected literally whilst the private view was going on as the new price list was lost somehow within a few minutes of the original one being used.

For the opening, the harbour master had provided a live band, playing some fine, mellow Cosmo jazz.

Whilst this was going on, I was saying hello to the people who had come. Our son and little sister were present and the show was in full bloom.

That evening was spectacular for me as I rarely sell, although I have sold personally for 30 years, but never in public galleries, only in my own shows.

That evening I was happy as I had sold more than I realised. I tried to recall it.

Although there were two long tables, the centrepiece and a small table with tools, rocks, rare metals, etcetera, it was the centrepiece that I remember the most.

A lot of the marble and ceramics were sold on the first night. By the end of the show, including paintings, I took back to Dartmoor maybe a third of the works.

So it shows you can do it.

All the money that I made was distributed, i.e. rents, bills, kids. The rest I needed for a new pair of boots and not second-hand ones, so this was a treat...

Although they had long gone, they lasted two years and then began to loosen. I took them to the shop to get them sorted. On collection, I asked the man, "How long will these boots last?"

He said, "Not long – no stitching, you see – it's all glue. If you want a good pair you have to go London – no money here."

I laughed. I knew what he meant.

Well, the next day, I looked down and a fish mouth was looking up at me.

A vex, mi juss pay dis raas man nuff shekki, an im gimmi fish mout.

Well a vex, kiss me few teet an gaan a wuk...

On the way, I stopped at another cobbler and asked if they had anything just to keep the rain out from the fish mouth.

Well, the lady took the fish mouth, put him 'pon a spinning machine and put a glue in there.

Fish mout gaan, get ship out...

Back to work...

When I put my hand in the water to pick up a rock, it's always deeper than it looks.

Even in the shallows...

THE RURAL WAYS... FANTASY

For most of my time working it has been in rural locations, living amongst local people, and in harmony with nature.

The pace of life suits me well. As an adult I reflect upon my rural youth and the steady gaze of wonder is always present.

The setting is not a cultural base, it is an ever-changing abstract, in musical frequencies...

The evergreen landscape, worn buckets, hedgerows, barking dogs, calling birds and, yes, cow and horse shit.

The long steep winding lanes. The wonder has no name... simple things are great.

Nettle is king and gossip queen.

Now let it be said,

Our toil is just, likewise the beaver.

Who can recall a day of dance and merry?

STUDIO LIFE

It was only when I began to sell from my own shows that things got better as I had to pay bills in order to have a place to work. I have had workspaces for the past 30 years and have created a studio trail of where I have worked in Devon and Cornwall.

Within these 30 years of studio-hopping I have met some interesting local people living there.

I am fond of the local ways.

The people who live off the tracks, etcetera.

I feel they are close to the earth in similar ways.

~

Since the issues with the police, I feel exposed in Devon now.

It's only the elements that help.

Although I am very pleasant and have manners, I still feel out of place with most things.

Sometimes I feel too exposed being here with some of the places and the people.

I never thought I would feel this about a rural setting, but I do, so I stay elemental.

Back to school but as an adult...

THE VISIT

In 2002, along with my younger brother, we took the bus to the school, way out in the sticks. When we got off the bus everything came flooding back.

But it was okay.

Then we had the long drive to walk. It's about a mile and a half.

When using the drive as a child, I would always look at the fields in season as that's all there was.

But this was enough as I became familiar with it all.

The earth, soil, crop, harvest, as each field would change colour depending on what was being grown.

The cornfield was one I remember going into. There were narrow paths in them that would go to the other end. Sometimes we would sit inside them and just talk or be quiet.

There were some younger children than our age. Some were aged 9 upwards. As I befriended one, I became aware of the younger ones as they were so small, almost fragile.

THE DORMITORY

I think we went to bed at 7.30 to 8.00 pm depending on age.

There were three large dormitories, maybe 20 beds in each one.

We would wash or shower, clean our teeth and then change into pyjamas, then into bed.

The light was left on for maybe an hour, then just a corridor light with the door wide open.

One teacher always did night duty. I knew as a few nights I would go to the toilet and see a teacher reading a book or just sitting still.

We never spoke unless we needed something.

I remember we talked quietly until we were fast asleep.

~

Now, walking up that long path 30 years later with my younger brother, because it was quite a long walk, I had time to reflect upon the atmosphere around us.

As we approached, one had to walk carefully across the cattle grid.

Sometimes I would leap across it as I was good at sport, especially running.

I could run for miles and not get tired.

When I ran, I was gone, literally, mentally, in all ways.

Anyway...

Once across the grid, I embraced it all.

The vast giant cedars were still majestic. I used to peel the bark in summer as I liked the smell.

I saw the boys running, walking, laughing, crying, teachers, smells, then back to my quiet brother who was taking it all in.

The new owner had turned the property into holiday lettings.

The dormitories were divided up.

He asked me if I had attended the school.

I told him yes and when and that this was my first time back since leaving.

I introduced my brother, then we had another chat.

Because I was not invited to look around and I didn't feel able to ask, I accepted our encounter with warmth. He asked me where I lived and that was that. I thanked him and left.

My brother doesn't say much but he did recall coming to visit with mum when around 7 or 8 years old.

I remember the trip and showing them our dormitory, which my brother liked.

It was always like a tingle of wonder when I beheld her face.

Those Mayal medicine women know too much.

But silent they are.

You are expected to interpret to the point of boil…

And this is how Mother was.

Just like her mother.

And her mother before that.

Medicine women of the constellation.

~

I remember staying with my real grandmother deep in Jamaica below the blue mountains.

…Ma P is a true community medicine woman who lived in a communal yard with one tap in the middle.

You could sit there all day and watch the dramas and activity around this tap.

I laughed a lot.

The one-room cabin was divided by a curtain and a large mattress I shared with my 3 younger cousins.

My grandmother and the two girls shared a bed.

But a share of their floor space, I noticed, was for a flat bed for sick people, and when I looked properly the room doubled as a healing room full of roots medicine.

In fact, whilst I stayed, a sick boy came for 10 days as his mother couldn't afford anything so Ma P treated the boy.

All I remember was a boy, say aged 6.

He was laid on that flat bed and soon Ma P got to work.

I saw these huge leaves being steamed continually and herbs being rubbed onto the boy. It looked like he had a high fever.

After this tonics were boiled and sipped, 10 days later that boy was out in the sun playing football.

~

My great grandparents from my mother's side were white landowners.

And my great grandfather worked on their land as the main blacksmith.

The daughter of that family and my great grandfather had a relationship and she had a child, my grandfather, who when born was adopted, given a new name with land and a little money.

My grandmother who married him told me he was depressed when he found out about his real mother, who he never met.

My mother never mentioned the story to me.

But she did have a healthy relationship with her father, who I never met, but I saw pictures of him when I was young.

I asked my mother who he was and she said, "He was your grandfather."

The first thing I noticed was that he looked Spanish or mixed race, but that was just an observation.

~

In 2009 whilst working in my former studio...

I had this sensation in my stomach. I felt heavy, like a presence was within me.

At first I kept it at bay – then slowly a lady began to visualise. She looked like Virginia Wolf but with a softer face.

She was so heavy with grief I had to fully embrace her...

This was my great grandmother.

Calling herself Clara.

She had come to tell me all her life story and to translate this information into an installation of her life.

It was an autobiographical collaborative works, and the deeper I got the more she revealed about her life in the 1800s.

I was so involved at one point I thought I too was going to pass out, but she promised to take care of me as the work was deep.

It was all white materials, almost sterile clinical works – lots and lots of it, but all in shades of sterile white.

The materials were: wood - jute - plaster - felt - latex - rope - white paint - wire mesh - white lace-sand - chalk.

Most if not all the pillars were carved in some way or other, having a decomposed maternal presence, but it was all one body of work which I exhibited once and have put away for another space to exhibit.

Even the titles of each individual piece had an eerie feel to them, like pillars of skin and an unknown sender.

Some of the pillars were 3 metres tall.

With lots of smaller sculptures, there would have been over a hundred sculptures in total.

It was during the last few months of completion I asked to see the parents.

Now, you must remember I am in my studio, and I ask to see her parents.

Before I finish the sentence, I am standing in front of the parents in an 1800s house in the West Indies.

But I did not take them in. First, I took in the kitchen: utensils - curtains - windows - sink...

And then the parents.

It was odd because, as I stood before them, again I took in their 19th century attire, then the parents.

The mother looked very indignant. Her daughter had disgraced the family and the mother had washed her hands of her daughter completely.

The father had a look of resignation. He looked like he had done the worst thing possible and carried a burden.

The second I comprehended this, I was back in the studio.

By now the work was almost complete and I felt this great relief as her weight became light and she was gone.

I felt this strong release. At last she was free.

So this is how I got to know about my Caucasian great grandmother – on my mother's side.

These same traits I saw in Mother – a strong sense of other, which seems genetic.

Back to school...

At school, I remember Miss Mary...

A tiny lady who only seemed to drink warm water.

Miss Mary had a strong benign presence. I was always aware of her presence as she spoke very clearly but quietly. She had large, resigned eyes like a mother with a newborn.

You could feel her focus.

I silently learnt a lot from Miss Mary, which was an inner stillness she moved with whenever we spoke. I always left with her presence on me.

~

Miss Rose was a very fine teacher. She was different in her own way and seemed to fully enjoy being with us.

I did notice that Miss Rose was brown.

It was Miss Rose who helped me when my wrist was in plaster. I can remember Miss Rose dressing me, making my bed and helping in any way possible. Plus Miss Rose had a beautiful face, when I recall her now.

One time, Miss Rose took us ice-skating in the minibus.

Suddenly we went through a deep puddle of water that sprayed the bus and made this incredible oval shape on either side of the bus. We all held our breath then laughed...

~

I was approaching 15 and suddenly I felt I wasn't attached to the school any more.

An awareness of being in this special residential school really took shape – my first so-called identity presence.

I realised the school I attended was for special needs children – this invisible badge was now visible...

...and I was it.

This created a conundrum pour moi.

I decided to just keep moving.

I realised that it was going to be something, but I was confident to step into it...

The land of no-no.

It felt right – I was giving birth. I was in labour.

This labour was a ballad by, say, Brook Benton.

Or even Labi Siffre, who mentioned Ella Fitzgerald.

Well, I can assure you, with these influences / frequencies, something happened...

I heard the original Wailers' 'Mellow Mood'...

'It hurts to be alone, sitting in the park waiting for yoooooooooooooooo.'

That was it laid low by high culture, never to stand again in the former ways.

The culture now was coming from a global perspective and I was free to find out in my own way and essence...

I travelled a lot, just moving, but having good experiences, with the elements by my side, and within my eyes a little more was revealed of the inner kingdom...

As too much of anything.

CANDY GIRL

The famous glamour model from the 8th Century came out of the Shitty.

Really?

ANTI COCO

You're really wanting for me to be black?

You mean not in skin colour but how I behave?

A few tests, you say?

No, definitely can't dance like that...

Final notes on 'Jast a thaaght'...

Yes we see her sometimes and wonder.

I wouldn't tell her like that child did.

How did she take it?

THE SCENE...

The child is in a residential street.

It is quiet for the Shitty, then it is only 10 am.

They don't get up till 4pm.

The child is on an errand and sees the woman near a doorway coming out from it as if leaving a shop, walking out slowly.

As he approaches to pass, meeting her leaving the doorway, the woman says, "Jast a Thaaght."

To whom?

To whom did she say it to?

Was it the person in the shop she had come out of?

The child thought she was talking to him as there was no one else about.

ACTION...

Woman: *"Jast a Thaaght."*

Child: *"Why yu talkin like that – it's not posh, and I'm tellin' Mami."*

At this point we are lost.

According to Mami, they did not speak anything else, as the child states...

The woman simply walked into the future...

And finally...

The part of the book I avoided...

It's a test.

A Kit test.

Okay, it's an imbecile home test kit.

I just needed to find out, as it comes and goes, the need to know...

So here goes...

Deep breath...

The word 'Insultar' in Spanish means 'to insult'.

To an Imbo... the interpretation means what?

Is there salt in it?

And, as you can see, I pass with triumphant disappointment, and no longer need to keep commenting on the labels given.

Farewell Imbecile – you served your purpose.

I will never forget you, for in many ways you gave me something I can share, and that's wonderful to know.

So, Imbo...

Do you mind the term Imbo?

Got it.

Got what?

A raincoat...

RHYTHM AND BODIES OF WORK

Since starting out in my work the first thing I noticed was the ways these bodies of work want to be exhibited. I thought it was plinth works, but this was installation. The works came in bodies, or series of works.

Not all, but most, and although the themes varied, the Atavist presence in the works was fixed...

As then, alongside ceramics, I did large, freestanding sculptures for both outdoor and inside. The materials used are varied, working upon multiple bodies of work as close to one another as possible...

Like musical scores, the bodies of works evolved.

There was a rhythm in the bodies of works. Everything seemed to fall into place.

For example, in 2010 we had a mean winter, but a beautiful one.

In a rural setting where I prefer to work, I like the way snow silences everything and you get a light tinge of pink from the evening winter sun.

I worked that winter on a body of works called Ocho Casas [Eight Houses]. This was physical work, with piles and piles of wooden beams of all sizes.

Within the six months from October to March this large body of work emerged in my studio with an inside temperature of minus 17 degrees. With no heat, this was my home. What did I eat to keep warm? Raw ginger.

What were the themes behind Ocho Casas?

The body of work was to do with our psychological being, the internal being in conflict with the outer being, which to a degree needs material requirements. This is the overload, the issue attachment, claimant, ownership, protective.

All material and physical matter, recorded in the daily frequencies, remind us maybe less is more.

Let me ask a Jamaican...

Ah, here's one coming. What a walk he's got.

Yes I, is which paart ah yard yu ail fram?

No, tell me, ah Kingston mon, nuh tru?

Martinique, is Martinique I, from – French leegro.

Cacafaat, weh dat?

Carib ocean blue, me brotha.

But yu look like wi.
Even di raas walk yu du deh straight outa Bull Bay gully.

Mek wi goh a bar an taalk likkle...

THE JAMAICAN

Mi name Herman from di Blue Mountan regin.
Mi full name Herman Jerome Francis.
Mi have 3 bredda an 5 sista.
Mi pupa ah faama man ah sell friut weh im grow.
Nuff man wuk deh faarm deh.
Well when mi reach aig seven mi buk up pon ah breeze.
Mi muma shout out wata wata an di breeze gaan.
Prees cyaan ovastan dem mystri deh.
Ah sciance mi French bredda.

But wait, which paart ah yu is French?

Gaston. My name is Gaston from de nordern paart ov Maartiniiqe. We are in de region of Mont Pele, a place call Le Lorrain, but we call it Segge Po.

Yes, I also have a big family of 5 and I am in the middle.
We Martiniquans respect Jamaicans.

The music from that island is global. It's good music and we, the rest of the Caribe, love Jamaica for this.

Is cool, mi bredda, cah ah wah evribadi ah taak bout shitty green an ow shitty tun eena western movie, gun ruuule mi bredda, ah di gun ting yu nuh.

But mi nuh waan bada yu wid dat.

What's yu take on physcological baggage?

Gaston, yu meen esclave?

Herman, dat ah mental genocide ta raas.

Gaston, with respect to the past, our culture is not just a word; it 'as its place in both worlds. Our Ancestors are never wrong. This is why it is important to have self-control in all things, this is what the Ancestors say.

The past too is a word conjuring images of places and peoples that are somehow part of us when in fact it is we – we are the past, present and future, if you know what I mean.

Herman, Mr Martinique, what ah speeech, what ah wurd smit yu tun owt tu be, an so eloquent...

Weh ya du ova ya?

Yu ah student?

Ar tourist?

Well, yes a tourist on business.

I'm opening up a music venue here in Hammersmith.

Playing and cooking always go together.

By the way, Herman, do you know of any sculptors?

Sculpta – yu mean barba shop?

Luckily Gaston didn't get the mix up but soon realised that Herman was on his own level.

"Pass by sometime." Gaston gave Herman a card and left. Printed on it read the words 'Segge Po' – past, present, future venues.

~

In 2010 I also did a body of work called Artificial Hunger – 1 of 4...

The materials were plastic - bones - metal. It was just over a metre in height.

The varied plastic had to be melted over the bone armature, which was a smelly job, never to be achieved again, but the pieces had a potent message...

A lady who saw them broke down and said they reminded her of the holocaust.

That was not the intention, which I think she knew.

The theme was plastics and synthetics impacts on both land and aquatic life.

Also in the clothing, food and skin industry, and the natural food cycles becoming out of kilter, being replaced with artificial hunger.

This artificial hunger is no joke – it will completely turn you inside out.

One would not recognise oneself if there was a proper food shortage...

PORN, TOO GOOD TO BE TRUE

Shirley, better known as Sherl, was a very busy person.

She was into art suddenly, even purchasing a gallery, and now scouting for artists...

The 1st four were in, but the 5th?

She said, "It's knickers he wants."

He said, "Where's the edit button?"

Now it's power.

...Knickers power.

That nicka bitch stay clear of me.

I know your sort, and if not,

I'm telling Mami.

I'm going indoors and telling Mami.

Mamiii.

Mamiii.

Mami comin'.

I called her.

"Mami," I said, "is knickers allowed?"

"Allowed where, son?"

"Up the arse, Mami – I seen them jaspers with vibrators on the internet."

Mami turned purple and chased me, and I ran and ran and hid under a bridge. Mami came to the bridge and just stopped. She was so still and quiet I had to come from under the bridge, and so I did.

Mamii.

Mamii.

Mamii.

"Why yu lips so big?"

"Cos I'm Amazonian and eat honey!"

Later Mami had a talk with me about the earlier talk...

"You say you see it on the internet."

"Yes Mami, everyone does."

Mami was staring at me, a strange frequency filled the space and I felt vacant, empty, almost echoey. I was afraid to move as I stared at Mami.

All these images came to me from the Internet and they seemed to be made of foam. Soon I was myself and never saw these again.

Q. You seem to answer questions with questions to end a sentence. Where does this idea come from, as this also seems to work?

A. Mami would answer questions with questions, *don't it?*

So from this sprang the offshoot – What do I mean?

Endings...

A FINAL VISIT TO SCHOOL 1981

I'm sitting on the lawn in front of the school, the year 1981.

The atmosphere seems transitional as the children move about. There's a scratch on my knee and as I study it Nicolas bumps into me as I roll onto the warm summer grass.

Some of us are chatting together. One friend suggests that the world isn't actually spinning, another states he wants to make his own thoughts out of magnets, and I said the Internet is coming...

~

Good afternoon, Mr Hooper. How are you and the family? It's been a while – over 35 years.

Could I quickly see Miss Mary, the holy one, or that nun that took me in?

Oh look how the fox hasn't changed.

My black leather shoes look vintage now, and my two front teeth are still Maasi...

~

"Jarvis, look – there's that orange bird I told you about."

JARVIS: "Strange feet."

"It's still a bird."

JARVIS: "Seen them in cartoon books, didn't know they were real. After all these years it's back, looking just the same."

"Don't you see, Jarvis, this time we're in is of no significance to that bird; it hasn't changed one bit."

JARVIS: "That's because it lives in the mind."

"Yes, but you saw it, didn't you? Even commenting on its feet."

JARVIS: "The mind did it."

"What mind?"

JARVIS: "The magnet..."

~

Pleeese may I see Maurice, just look at him from the corridor? Thank you, Mr Hooper, for your care and help.

I have to go now, Mr Hooper – the future calls...

A thought...

This ripping-off of artists is evident on the island of Jamaica. In the 1970s, 9 out of 10 artists got ripped off – as evident in the iconic culture film 'The Harder They Come' starring Jimmy Cliff who sang 'Many Rivers to Cross'.

The great Louis Armstrong sang 'What a Wonderful World'.

And Nesta sang, *'O mocking bird have you ever heard words that are never heard...'*

~

I feel to close this book with a compelling reality of the domesticated human...

THE EVOLUTION OF FREMBE – THE NOT SO GREAT...

HAVE YOU, YOU, YOU

EVER, EVER, EVER ASKED YOURSELF

WHEN MAN FIRST CAGED MAN?

TAMED MAN?

NOT THE BEAST, BUT MAN?

TAMED HIS LAND

TAMED HIS THOUGHTS

TAMED HIS SOIL

TAMED HIS BULLY

TAMED HIS SWEAT

TAMED HIS SURVEILLANCE

TAMED HIS POSE

TAMED HIS CULTURE

TAMED HIS MANNERISM

TAMED HIS CREATIVITY

TAMED HIS KHAKI

TAMED HIS BIRTH CERTIFICATE

TAMED HIS TWEED

TAMED HIS SEXUALITY

TAMED HIS HYPOCRISY

TAMED HIS GOLD MINES

TAMED HIS PRIVACY

TAMED HIS WEALTH

TAMED HIS KEYS

TAMED HIS HOUSE

TAMED HIS PISS

TAMED HIS COMING IN, GOING OUT

TAMED HIS TV

TAMED HIS BELIEFS

TAMED HIS LANGUAGE

TAMED HIS DNA

TAMED HIS HUT

TAMED HIS LAPTOP

TAMED HIS CELEBRITY

TAMED HIS SENTENCE

TAMED HIS REBELLION

TAMED HIS SPEAR

TAMED HIS PHONE

TAMED HIS EDUCATION

TAMED HIS ILLUSION

TAMED HIS SOCIETY

TAMED HIS GENDER

TAMED HIS CLOUDS

TAMED HIS NYAM NYAM

TAMED HIS FRIENDSHIP

TAMED HIS PRESCRIPTION

TAMED HIS SPERM

TAMED HIS IOU

TAMED HIS ANGER – WITH DRUGS

TAMED HIS BANK

TAMED HIS SLAVES

TAMED HIS STEPS

TAMED HIS CONDOM

TAMED HIS ISM

TAMED HIS SCHISM

TAMED HIS SHOES

TAMED HIS WINE

TAMED HIS FREEDOM

TAMED HIS FOOD

TAMED HIS BRAWL

TAMED HIS SAMPLE

TAMED HIS SPIES

TAMED HIS DEMOCRACY

TAMED HIS FASCISM

TAMED HIS STEP MOM

TAMED HIS IGLOO

TAMED HIS NOSE

TAMED HIS FORWARD MARCH

TAMED HIS PLEASE

TAMED HIS MISCONCEPTION

TAMED HIS CLOTHES

TAMED HIS CLIMATE

TAMED HIS WALK

TAMED HIS GREAT, GREAT, GREAT GRANDFATHER

TAMED HIS TALK

TAMED HIS CORRUPTION

TAMED HIS HABITUAL LIE TO TRUTH

TAMED HIS GOON SQUAD

TAMED HIS VOICE

TAMED HIS PROPAGANDA

TAMED HIS BIOLOGICAL WARS

TAMED HIS FOOLS

TAMED HIS PLANS

TAMED HIS NEWS

TAMED HIS VICTORY

TAMED HIS CRACK

TAMED HIS MEMORY

TAMED HIS GROOVE

TAMED HIS TANK

TAMED HIS SPORT

TAMED HIS VICAR

TAMED HIS WEATHER

TAMED HIS CADETS

TAMED HIS WATER

TAMED HIS PROTEST

TAMED HIS VASELINE ASS

TAMED HIS FREEDOM

TAMED HIS TEETH

TAMED HIS PSYCHO

TAMED HIS ALIBI

TAMED HIS MUSIC

TAMED HIS TRAITS

TAMED HIS MARRIAGE

TAMED HIS DIVORCE

TAMED HIS BILL

TAMED HIS FRUIT

TAMED HIS VEG

TAMED HIS EJACULATION

TAMED HIS KIDS

TAMED HIS CO-HOST

TAMED HIS BLUES

TAMED HIS MASTURBATION

TAMED HIS MOON WALK

TAMED HIS TEARS

TAMED HIS KINDNESS

TAMED HIS ADVERTS

TAMED HIS DECEITS

TAMED HIS RHYTHM

TAMED HIS JOY

TAMED HIS SOLITARY CONFINEMENT

TAMED HIS SLACK

TAMED HIS LOOT

TAMED HIS ENGINE

TAMED HIS TRACTOR

TAMED HIS VACCINE

TAMED HIS SHADOW

TAMED HIS DANCE

TAMED HIS HISTORY

TAMED HIS PRESS

TAMED HIS ECONOMIC EXISTENCE

TAMED HIS PERVERSE

TAMED HIS PENIS GROWTH

TAMED HIS RAIN FOREST

TAMED HIS RIVERS

TAMED HIS CONTRACT

TAMED HIS LAND GRAB

TAMED HIS WEALTH

TAMED HIS ARTEFACTS

TAMED HIS MUSEUM

TAMED HIS FAME

TAMED HIS HISTORY

TAMED HIS AFTERSHAVE

TAMED HIS SNIPER

TAMED HIS BADGE

TAMED HIS FANATICS

TAMED HIS DOCILITY

TAMED HIS BIT ON THE SIDE

TAMED HIS BASTARDS

TAMED HIS TRIP

TAMED HIS TROP

TAMED HIS HIP HOP

TAMED HIS BITCHES

TAMED HIS ILLNESS

TAMED HIS WALLPAPER

TAMED HIS BENEFIT

TAMED HIS VOTE

TAMED HIS PAVEMENTS

TAMED HIS CACA [POO]

TAMED HIS SURRENDER

TAMED HIS ARTERIES

TAMED HIS GANG

TAMED HIS COLLAR

TAMED HIS CAMOUFLAGE

TAMED HIS BAIL

TAMED HIS MERCY

TAMED HIS OPPRESSION

TAMED HIS ANKLES

TAMED HIS BELIEF

TAMED HIS DEVIL

TAMED HIS ZOO

TAMED HIS TEACHERS

TAMED HIS SENSATION

TAMED HIS BROAD CHEST

TAMED HIS SECRETS

TAMED HIS DISPOSITION

TAMED HIS WAR

TAMED HIS SADISM

TAMED HIS HYPE

TAMED HIS VICTIMS

TAMED HIS EGO

TAMED HIS VET

TAMED HIS SONGS

TAMED HIS FLAG

TAMED HIS EXISTENCE

TAMED HIS WEAPON

TAMED HIS YESTERDAY, TODAY AND TOMORROW

TAMED HIS QUEST

TAMED HIS NATIONALISTIC JELLY TALK

TAMED HIS BEER

TAMED HIS FREQUENCY

TAMED HIS FIST

TAMED HIS BLAST OFF

TAMED HIS LUST

TAMED HIS DOG...

~

HAVE YOU, YOU, YOU

EVER, EVER, EVER ASKED YOURSELF

WHEN WOMAN WAS FIRST CAGED BY WOMAN?

NOT A BEAST BUT WOMAN?

TAMED HER SPACE

TAMED HER TEMPLE

185

TAMED HER DESIRES

TAMED HER INSTINCTS

TAMED HER STREETS

TAMED HER LABOUR PAINS

TAMED HER PLATOON

TAMED HER SHOPPING

TAMED HER COUGH

TAMED HER BUSH

TAMED HER DRUGS

TAMED HER NAILS

TAMED HER ORGASM

TAMED HER SPITE

TAMED HER WONDERINGS

TAMED HER GENDER

TAMED HER SENSUALITY

TAMED HER TAN

TAMED HER JOBS

TAMED HER CALMNESS

TAMED HER HOLIDAYS

TAMED HER GUISE

TAMED HER DIESEL

TAMED HER LICENCE

TAMED HER WHEELS

TAMED HER TOY BOY

TAMED HER PRE SCHOOL

TAMED HER WEALTH

TAMED HER IMMUNE SYSTEM WITH DRUGS

TAMED HER STRANGE LIPS

TAMED HER QUESTIONS

TAMED HER PRIVACY

TAMED HER DREAMS

TAMED HER ADVERTS

TAMED HER FETISH

TAMED HER KNICKERS

TAMED HER STRAP-ON

TAMED HER BALLADS

TAMED HER TOUCH

TAMED HER PROOF

TAMED HER HIPS

TAMED HER SNAKE

TAMED HER MOONS

TAMED HER GIN

TAMED HER SORROW

TAMED HER SCENTED CANDLES

TAMED HER BULLETS

TAMED HER STRONG ARM

TAMED HER NOBLE BACK

TAMED HER ESSENCE

TAMED HER JASPER

TAMED HER DIRECTION

TAMED HER EYES

TAMED HER SURRENDER

TAMED HER WOMANHOOD

TAMED HER FRUITS

TAMED HER WONDER

TAMED HER BIRTH

TAMED HER FUTURE

TAMED HER CRIES

TAMED HER BOOKS

TAMED HER PASSIONS

TAMED HER NO, NO

TAMED HER RAGE

TAMED HER GOOGLE SEARCH

TAMED HER VOICE

TAMED HER INSTINCT

TAMED HER QUESTIONING

TAMED HER MORNING AFTER PILL

TAMED HER ROOTS

TAMED HER DISPLACEMENT

TAMED HER HUSBAND'S FRIENDS

TAMED HER POSSIBILITIES

TAMED HER EDUCATION

TAMED HER PROMISE

TAMED HER WALK

TAMED HER FASHION

TAMED HER TALK

TAMED HER PANTS

TAMED HER BAIT

TAMED HER FABRICS

TAMED HER GRACE

TAMED HER SWAY

TAMED HER STEADY

TAMED HER BREASTS

TAMED HER PAST

TAMED HER STRENGTHS

TAMED HER LOVE

TAMED HER PRESERVES

TAMED HER CAUTION

TAMED HER FRAGRANCE

TAMED HER GARDEN

TAMED HER SWEETNESS

TAMED HER TOUCH

TAMED HER FENCE

TAMED HER BELL

TAMED HER MOOD – WITH DRUGS

TAMED HER ALARM

TAMED HER CORN

TAMED HER LOOK

TAMED HER OVAL

TAMED HER BREED

TAMED HER NATURAL WIG

TAMED HER PRAMS

TAMED HER BEARD

TAMED HER MEDICAL RECORDS

TAMED HER GOODWILL

TAMED HER NEW YOU

TAMED HER CLOSE UP

TAMED HER DUMMIES

TAMED HER PORN

TAMED HER IMPLANTS

TAMED HER HUNGER

TAMED HER NATURAL HIPS

TAMED HER NATURAL VOICE

TAMED HER TAM TAM

TAMED HER POSTURE

TAMED HER POWER

TAMED HER HALLELUJAH

TAMED HER FREAK

TAMED HER MEDICINE

TAMED HER CRADLE

TAMED HER NAVAL

TAMED HER MUD

TAMED HER SEEDS

TAMED HER TWIST

TAMED HER WISDOM

TAMED HER LICK

TAMED HER CONSTELLATION

TAMED HER WEATHER

TAMED HER TRICKS

TAMED HER BASIS

TAMER HER SELF

TAMED HER SACRED

TAMED HER FOUNDATION

TAMED HER NAKED

TAMED HER CREDIT CARD

TAMED HER DEMON

TAMED HER NEW BORN

TAMED HER LOW FREQUENCY

TAMED HER DREAMS

TAMED HER CENTRE

TAMED HER JUDGE

TAMED HER STENCH

TAMED HER PUSSY LICKING

TAMED HER PURPLE BRUISE

TAMED HER PLASTIC ASS

TAMED HER PRAYER

TAMED HER MIRRORS AND WINDS...

~

Thank you for taking time to read this book.
The fact that it is now in print is a great release,
an exhalation...

Paul Devon Young, 2021
amagaceramics@gmail.com

~

I am compiling an anthology of short stories and poems.

To order a copy or for inspirational talk,
please contact the above email.

Printed in Great Britain
by Amazon